TRAINING DOGS
A Manual

TRAINING DOGS

A Manual

COLONEL KONRAD MOST

*Translated from the German
by James Cleugh*

London
POPULAR DOGS

POPULAR DOGS PUBLISHING CO. LTD

178–202 Great Portland Street, London W1

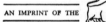

AN IMPRINT OF THE   HUTCHINSON GROUP

London Melbourne Sydney
Auckland Bombay Toronto
Johannesburg New York

ABRICHTUNG DES HUNDES

Individuell und ohne Strafen

12th Edition published in Germany 1951

TRAINING DOGS

A Manual

First published in Great Britain August 1954
Reprinted November 1955
Reprinted January 1957
Reprinted November 1958
Reprinted January 1960
Reprinted November 1962
Reprinted July 1964
Reprinted September 1966
Reprinted August 1968

*This book has been set in Old Style, printed in Great Britain
on Antique Wove paper by Anchor Press,
and bound by Wm. Brendon, both of Tiptree, Essex.*

09 045612 2

ACKNOWLEDGMENT

The publishers are indebted to Dr. Eric Fitch Daglish and Mr. John Holmes for much help and advice in the production of this book. The photographs taken by Howard Evans were specially staged for this book by Mr. Holmes with his dogs.

KONRAD MOST

A Biographical Note

COLONEL MOST was one of the world's most experienced and distinguished authorities on all types of dog training and a pioneer in the study of dog psychology. He started training Service dogs in 1906 while serving as Police Commissioner at the Royal Prussian Police Headquarters, Saarbrücken. For the next eight years he gave instruction to the Constabulary on the training and management of police dogs for all purposes by methods evolved by himself. In 1912 he was appointed Principal of the newly formed State Breeding and Training Establishment for police dogs at Berlin and carried out much original research in training dogs for Service personnel and for the tracking of criminals.

At the outbreak of war in 1914, Konrad Most was attached to the Staff of Field Marshal von Hindenburg, Commander-in-Chief in the East, to organize and direct the use of Army dogs on the Eastern Front, and the following year was put in charge of the organization of all canine services on both the Eastern and Western Fronts. In recognition of his war service he was, in 1919, awarded a testimonial by the Prussian War Ministry inscribed: "To Capt. Most, creator of the Canine Service in the World War of 1914–18." From 1919 to 1937 he was head of the Canine Research Department of the Army High Command, and during that period also acted as adviser to the Government of Finland on the organization of the Finnish Canine Services. He played a leading part in the formation of the Canine Research Society and of the German Society for Animal Psychology, both founded in 1931, and in 1938 was elected Honorary Life Member of both bodies in recognition of his work on their behalf.

From 1944 to 1947 Colonel Most was head of the Experimental Department at the Tutorial and Experimental Institute or Armed Forces' Dogs and Technical Principal of the North

German Dog Farm, a centre for the training of working dogs, their handlers and the trainers of dogs for the blind. In 1951 he became closely associated with courses held in the Rhine Palatinate for the instruction of sportsmen in the training and management of hunting and tracking dogs for the purpose of improving their performances in the field.

In 1954 – the year of his death, aged 76 – Colonel Most was awarded an Honorary Doctorate of the Justus-Liebig Technical College, Giessen, Hesse, near Frankfurt-am-Main. His manual *Training Dogs*, first written in 1910, is the recognized standard work on the subject throughout Europe.

CONTENTS

Author's Introduction   *Page* 13

PART I

THE THEORY OF TRAINING

I. BASIC PRINCIPLES: The Way to Mutual Understanding between Man and Dog   17

II. THE USE OF COMPULSION AND INDUCEMENTS   26

PART II

PRACTICAL TRAINING

III. ACTION AND ABSTENTION—ACCELERATION OF
PACE—DISCIPLINARY EXERCISES: Heel on lead;
Behaviour off the lead; Sitting   47

IV. DOWN AND RECALL EXERCISES: General;
Teaching the Down; Dropping on command   62

V. SPECIAL INSTRUCTIONS ON THE RECALL   71

VI. STANDING STILL—JUMPING   97

VII. REFUSAL OF FOOD AND CURE OF THE HABITS OF
EATING OR ROLLING IN REFUSE—RETRIEVING   102

VIII. DEFENCE WORK WITH THE GUARD DOG: General:
Self-defence of dog when alone; Man-work without protective clothing; Man-work in protective
clothing; So-called stick-sureness   123

9

IX. RECONNAISSANCE: General; Human Reconnaissance; Object Reconnaissance. TRACKING: Services available; General; Training the track-happy dog; Free tracking by the track-happy dog; Training the track-sure dog   154

X. FAMILIARIZATION WITH DISTURBANCES—WORK IN WATER—"SPEAKING"   192

XI. TRAINING AND MANAGEMENT OF SERVICE DOGS   198

Index   202

ILLUSTRATIONS

Working Collie at heel free	*Facing page* 48
Alsatian scaling a jump of 9 feet	48
Alsatian retrieving a Service revolver over a gorse hedge	49
Retrieving in water	49
Alsatian stands still while handler searches "criminal"	64
Alsatian jumps to protect handler	64
Man-work in full protective clothing	65
Alsatian arrests "criminal"	65
Dog baying "criminal" with stick	112
Dog baying but not attacking injured person	113
Dog on reconnaissance finds a hidden "criminal"	128
Leash tracking on a road	129

IN THE TEXT

Figs.		*Page*
1.	Heel on lead	53
2.	Heel on lead	53
3.		
4.	Wilhelm Busch's *Max and Moritz*	74
5.		75
6.		
7.	Running backwards from dog	83
8.	Visual signal to stand still	97
9.	First jumping exercises	101
10.	Dog snaps at the dumb-bell	111
11.	Position of dumb-bell in jaws	111

Figs.   *Page*

12. Transverse section of dog's neck   119

13. First hold for retrieving under compulsion   120

14. Second hold for retrieving under compulsion   120

15. Dog brought within snapping range of dumb-bell   121

16. Grasping skin of throat and fondling   121

17. Reconnaissance. A to E = handler's direction   155

18. Tracking up wind   165

19. Tracking down wind   166

20. A curving track   167

21. Wind blowing across track   168

22. Overshooting a fresh track   169

23. Böttger's track-harness   181

24. Starting a track   185

25. Example of track   188

26. Example of track   188

Author's Introduction to this Edition

From my early childhood I was strongly attracted to the study of nature and have always had a deep interest in and love for all animals, especially dogs. It was, therefore, natural that at the outset of my career as a police officer I should have been drawn to work with Service dogs.

When, many years ago, I took the first guard dog trained by me to a trial, the remarkable performance it put up aroused widespread interest, even among experienced trainers of long standing. After the trial I was asked by what method of training I had achieved such striking results and had to confess that I was unable to explain how I had done it. It was true, I said, that I had studied several textbooks on training, but, as I had been unable to accept the rules there laid down, I had, so to speak, unconsciously evolved a system of my own. Later I fell to considering again the various questions that had been put to me and reached the conclusion that they could be answered fully and correctly only after a study of psychology. I therefore set about the task of reading all the literature dealing with the subject that I could obtain, and came to realize that the method I had followed differed from others in that it was based on a form of training which treated the dog, not as an intelligent human pupil imbued with a sense of duty, but as an animal, beyond good or evil, living in a world without moral values and learning not by logical thinking but solely through the faculty of memory. The recognition of this basic principle was the origin of my training system as set out in the following pages.

This system avoids the mistake of endowing dogs with human understanding and morals; a mistake which renders any real partnership between man and dog so difficult. By the

13

methods described no demand exceeding its powers of comprehension are made on the dog. The animal is thus spared much suffering and the man much disappointment and annoyance; while the enjoyment of both pupil and trainer is facilitated and increased.

K. M.

1954.

Part 1

THE THEORY OF TRAINING

CHAPTER I

BASIC PRINCIPLES:

The Way to Mutual Understanding between Man and Dog

FROM childhood onwards we are taught a great deal that is wrong about the psychology of animals. In fables, fairy-tales and stories describing animal life and behaviour we are often presented with living beings that think, understand human speech and perform moral or immoral acts. If we adopt these anthropomorphic views we shall be at a disadvantage whenever we try to train animals of any kind, but particularly when we are dealing with dogs.

We can save ourselves much disappointment and ensure the dog's more rapid and cheerful response to instruction by allowing him to learn in the canine way.

The dog most closely resembles man in his emotional and instinctive reflexes. He is capable of showing his emotions very eloquently and his manner of expressing his feelings is clearly reflected in our own.

It is responses of this kind that largely account for our deep affection for dogs. We are so impressed by the acuteness of such senses as those of scent and hearing, and with the capacity to learn, that we are prone to assume that a dog's mental equipment approximates to our own. We credit him with capacity for thought and with an understanding of human behaviour and morality. By introducing the dog into a world which is, in reality, for ever closed to him, we prevent ourselves from recognizing the unbridgeable mental gap that exists between man and dog.

The instruction in training methods developed in the following pages is intended to serve as a guide to a system of teaching suited both to the emotional and to the instinctive life of the animal.

A dog's ability to grasp an idea resembles in certain respects that of an infant that has not yet learned to speak. Such a child is incapable of understanding any particular word spoken. One may, for instance, say to a recumbent child, "Get up." But the sound remains an empty echo that dies away without producing any response.

Let us suppose that an infant and a dog are to be photographed by time exposure. It will be impossible to explain the meaning of what is intended to either. They know nothing about photography or its requirements. They do not understand the request 'Keep still' whether it is spoken as a command or as an entreaty. We must, therefore, restrict ourselves to an appeal to the senses only. We may, for example, rattle something. This will, in many cases, arouse attention, and thus immobility, for a few moments. The conduct desired is, thereby, obtained without either the infant or the dog having the slightest idea of the intention of the photographer.

What happened when the rattling sound was made? Both heard a noise; an impression was made on their auditory senses. We call an impression of this kind a sense-stimulus, or simply a stimulus. Both man and dog possess five senses, if we keep to the five-fold division hallowed by tradition; they are: hearing, sight, scent, touch and taste. Each of these senses only responds to such stimuli as are appropriate to the special physical structure of each of the sense organs.

In the example cited we deliberately imposed a sense-stimulus upon both infant and dog, and it resulted in the reaction we expected.

In dealing with children or dogs we are restricted to the use of such external impressions. As soon as the infant masters human speech this situation changes, but it does not do so in the case of the dog.

Let us consider for a moment how the dog learns, in play, to fetch something. What sense-stimulus will cause the animal to seize the required object in its jaws? The answer to this question is: the movement of some object congenial to the dog immediately in front of him. By means of this we succeed in making the dog snap at the object, which becomes, from his point of view, a species of prey. This is the result of an inherited connection between the sense-stimulus denoting the escape of prey and the reaction resulting in pursuit and seizure.

But it is not sufficient if the dog merely snaps at such

objects, when we move them, and brings them to us. We want him to do this at an audible or visual signal; at a sense-stimulus corresponding with our purpose. But there is no inherited connection between such stimuli and seizure of the object. At this point, therefore, training begins. It consists in making the dog accustomed to behaving in certain ways as a result of deliberately imposed sense-stimuli based on memory. In order, for example, to teach the dog to retrieve, we employ, *at the same time* as the impression of a moving object, a further impression in the form of a sound, e.g. 'Fetch it.'

This auditory stimulus is, of course, wholly without effect to begin with. How does it happen, then, that the dog learns to snap at the object on receipt of the auditory stimulus 'Fetch it'? As already explained, this stimulus is always given simultaneously with a movement of the object. In this way the inherited association between the stimulus afforded by the escape movement of the ostensible prey and the reaction of snapping at it is reinforced, after a number of repetitions, by an association, induced by memory, between the auditory stimulus 'Fetch it' and the snapping action. As a result, the dog will then snap even when the sound 'Fetch it' is made without the addition of any other stimulus. At this point the sound is substituted for the moving object, and becomes the secondary inducement. Accordingly, we must distinguish between primary inducements as immediately creative of the action desired and secondary inducements; the latter become operative only when a memory-induced association between them and the behaviour we require is established.

It is not, however, always possible to make use of an inherited association as a basis for canine instruction. Nor can we always do so in the case of a child not yet able to speak. One may wish him, for instance, to raise both arms in response to the question, 'How big are you?' In such circumstances all one can do is to take both the child's arms, raise them, and at the same time rapidly ask the question. In this case the raising of the arms by the adult is the primary inducement given. After a number of repetitions the infant will one day raise its arms at the sound of the question alone, without any accompanying gesture by the adult. A memory-induced association has been established between auditory stimulus and movement.

The sound of the question has therefore become a 'secondary inducement'.

The raising of the child's arms, however, is to be distinguished from the primary inducements given by rattling something during photography or by moving an object in teaching a dog to fetch, by the fact that the arm-raising is at first brought about mechanically. The infant is treated like a puppet. One of the differences between puppet and child is that the latter possesses a brain and nerves, and that its nerves transmit to its brain the stimulus which comes with the raising of its arms. In training dogs many similar operations become necessary whenever behaviour in which inherited instincts can play little or no part is required. Primary inducements, therefore, are not restricted to simple sense-stimuli.

In the case of secondary inducements, however, we are always concerned with simple sense-stimuli; usually those of hearing and sight permitting control of the dog from a distance. The aim of training is to work upon the animal in such a way that he can eventually be relied upon to obey auditory or visual signs alone, in the absence of primary inducements.

It would, in theory, be perfectly possible to employ the senses of smell, taste or touch as secondary inducements. But there would be no point in doing so, since the object is not to train the working dog to act—e.g. to bark—on experiencing any particular scent, taste or touch of any part of its body.

In order to avoid the mistake of anthropomorphism when auditory stimuli are concerned, we should not speak of giving orders, but of uttering calls or other sounds and of making gestures when the stimuli concerned are visual. In individual exercises the various signals should be clearly distinguishable from one another. Auditory signals, moreover, should be made as brief and penetrating as possible. They should not be rendered as written words, but as sounds.

It cannot be too often repeated that there is but a purely external connection between these secondary inducements and the behaviour the dog comes to associate with them through an act of memory. A dog remembers only the temporal and spatial consequences of events, without grasping their connections as causes and effects. Still less does he understand the remoter aims we have in view when we induce him to initiate or suspend action. Nor is it necessary, for training purposes, that he should reach a higher level of comprehension.

As the dog is a far keener observer of movement than ourselves, the trainer must observe the following rules in making his own gestures or signals.

Let us assume that sufficient progress has been made in teaching the down to permit the trainer walking a few paces away from a dog left lying in the open. After taking a few steps he turns back and, as he turns, whistles for the animal. After a certain amount of repetition the dog will get up and come to the trainer as soon as the latter turns round, without waiting for the whistle. For the turning movement that has hitherto followed the call on every occasion has by this time come to mean the same thing to the dog as the whistle. The turning movement has become a secondary inducement, a visual signal for the recall. An *undesirable association has been established* between the turning round of the trainer and the signal to recall him. Undesirable associations are impeded by a separation in time of the events concerned. In the case under consideration the exercise must consist in the trainer first turning round, noticing that the dog is still lying down and then, after an interval, calling him.

In all such cases the trainer's gestures achieve the same effect as his audible signals and, therefore, anthropomorphically speaking, become 'commands', whenever certain auditory signals coincide in time with certain gestures. If the trainer is unaware of this fact, a whole series of undesirable associations will arise in the course of training and mistakes will ensue and be regarded as 'forgetfulness', 'disobedience', 'indifference', etc., on the part of the dog, with the result that he will be punished in error, with all the disadvantages thus entailed.

The question whether a dog should be trained to obey both sounds and gestures, or sounds alone, or gestures alone, depends upon the use to which the animal is to be put. Visual signals, for example, will not serve in complete darkness, but if silence is required, training in visual signals may, perforce, be an essential preliminary.

We have said that the dog cannot understand what we have in view in our use of him. But this fact should be clearly distinguished from the wider question whether animals have intelligence. This remains open to discussion. The question whether or not the dog employs intelligence and rudimentary thought in any human sense is not relevant to practical training. Experience in thousands of cases has proved that it is only training on a memory basis that can lead to reliable service. It is, therefore, necessary to make some remarks on the nature and power of memory.

The ability to retain in the mind what has been perceived, to take due note of it and reproduce or recall it, is known as memory. An experience is grasped by the memory as a whole. If a part of the experience is later undergone anew, its other parts automatically recur to consciousness. Thus, if we hear the words 'Silent night' or 'To be or not to be' or 'The curfew tolls', anyone who knows where these phrases occur and who has therefore always thought of the words referred to in connection with what follows, will immediately reproduce the words 'holy night', 'that is the question' or 'the knell of parting day', if not aloud, at any rate inwardly. The separate parts of what has been experienced become, so to speak, associated.

For practical purposes we deliberately establish such associations of ideas when we desire to remember anything particularly. If, for instance, we wish to remind ourselves to return a borrowed book, we may tie a knot in our handkerchief. When we notice the handkerchief again, perhaps while we are going to bed, and thus again perceive a part of what we have experienced in connection with it, that part reproduces its appendage, 'Return the borrowed book', through memory. As a rule, a single act of perception does not enable any related experience to be retained in the memory for very long: only a temporary, not a lasting, association has been formed. If one catches sight of the knotted handkerchief in the evening, one cannot always remember what it means. Repetitions are necessary if we desire to recollect something for a longish period; for instance, telephone numbers or a poem.

We must now proceed with our investigation of sense-stimuli and their consequences, in order to be able to understand the different way in which the dog, as contrasted with the adult human being, reacts to experience.

Hitherto we have only considered stimuli initiated by the trainer himself. A number of other stimuli remain to be studied. In some training exercises we make use of assistants. For example, those who play the part of criminals in the case of the guard dog. These assistants participate in the training. In collusion with ourselves they bring certain sense-stimuli to bear upon the dog to induce him to perform the actions we require. The dog, for example, may be irritated by the assistants, so that he may show hostility to them, or the assistant may run away, to get the dog to pursue him.

An important part is also played by the numerous sense-stimuli imposed on the dog by external conditions. Ignorance of such influences may cause undesirable associations to be formed, with refusal of the dog to act, and erroneous interpretations may be placed on such a refusal, which may in turn be succeeded by the adoption of erroneous measures for their correction. For instance: the trainer of a tracking-dog foresees the possibility of a culprit escaping across a ploughed field into a neighbouring wood and there climbing a tree. If this exercise is repeated several times and the dog is repeatedly given the *corresponding stimuli*, the visual stimulus of the visible track across the ploughed field causes the dog to become, contrary to the object of the training, accustomed to using the eye in tracking. The discovery of the assistant in a tree also causes, again contrary to the object of training, the sense-stimulus 'tree' to be transformed into a secondary stimulus 'person to be found'. Accordingly, the dog keeps his head up while tracking, on the look-out for footprints and trees along the trail, or else he actually leaves the track and runs off after any footprints or trees he may catch sight of.

We are here confronted by the extremely important question to what extent canine powers of understanding permit the animal to adapt his preliminary training in dealing with the real thing. The rule to be laid down is: the final aim of all training is to make every exercise as appropriate as possible to the ultimate service required. If, however, training for such a service, when repeated, leads to the formation of undesirable associations, it should be undertaken only rarely. It must, indeed, take place, in order to accustom the dog to stimuli which will occur when he takes up serious duty, but if it is found that training has formed undesirable associations it should be altogether avoided. If undesirable stimuli are produced during the actual performance of duty itself, the word must be 'go ahead', for there is nothing else to be done. It should be added, however, that a single experience does not by any means always establish an association. If it does, such an undesirable association may be dispersed, and thus withdrawn from the dog's memory, by further training.

Finally, a most important part is played by distractionary stimuli from external conditions. These are the distractions which almost always occur during the activity of the working dog on actual duty. The trainer of the working dog must take the greatest pains to introduce such distractions into the exercises performed in such a way as to guard against refusal by the dog when the real test comes. There is a fundamental difference here between common circus training, when only slight and invariably similar distractions are introduced during practice, and training for practical purposes, where the most variable and forcible interruptions that may occur on actual duty must be taken into consideration.

If only a dog's memory had to be considered while he was under instruction, successful training would be a very easy matter. As we know, however, the dog does not spontaneously perform all the services we require of him. We are often asked whether we should train a dog by kindness or compulsion. A kind heart is certainly an advantage to a trainer, but this alone will not induce the dog to perform reliable service, nor will treatment by those who are anthropomorphically inclined and who constantly see 'sullen resistance' on the part of the dog and inflict 'punishment' accordingly. Good training needs a kind heart as well as a cool and well-informed head for the proper direction of the indispensable compulsion.

What is the actual object of training? It is that the dog shall only do what we find convenient or useful, and refrain from doing what is inconvenient or harmful to us. This requirement cannot be completely reconciled with what is acceptable by, or of advantage to, the dog. A man often requires a dog to refrain from its natural activities or undertake those which are unnatural to it. Canine instincts, for example, prompt a dog to pursue, corner and catch prey, but not to bring it to a man. The aim of training can be achieved only by exercising compulsion whenever the dog does not spontaneously do what is required of him.

No one in ordinary circumstances drinks dirty water; but people will do so when they are tormented by thirst and there is nothing else to drink. Thirsty persons will even enjoy drinking dirty water. Under certain conditions, therefore, something disagreeable is done in order to avoid something still more disagreeable. The latter may be something so extremely unpleasant that it may compel the transformation of something unpleasant in itself into a positive pleasure. On the other hand it is possible for something agreeable to become disagreeable. A child loves playing with fire; but if it gets burnt it withdraws its finger. Why does a thirsty person drink filthy water? Why does a child refrain from its attractive game with fire? They have learnt that it is to their advantage to do so. It is only when a dog learns that the adoption or abandonment, disagreeable in themselves, of certain actions will be to his own advantage that training can be proceeded with on a sound basis. Such is the object of compulsion. A dog, too, will perform an uncongenial act, if it can thus avoid one still less congenial. He will stop doing something he likes if something disagreeable makes him dislike it. The animal has no idea of the service he renders to man by acting, or ceasing to act, for his own advantage. He has just as little understanding of the reason for his treatment by man. Nor are his acts or renunciations ethically directed. A dog cannot, therefore, in any true sense of the words be praised or blamed, rewarded or punished. We can only do something disagreeable or agreeable to him. It is also obviously pointless, in his case, to utter threats of future punishment.

A child that understands speech can be told to 'Come here!' The phrase is an order and is understood as such. If the child does not obey, it can be told, 'If you don't come, you'll get a smacking!' The child immediately realizes that it is being threatened by something disagreeable which it can avoid by obeying the previous order. This kind of realization is quite impossible in the case of a dog.

It is extremely important for us to be quite clear on this point. If our approach to training is based on moral ideas regarding punishment, reward, obedience, duty, etc., we are bound to handle the dog in the wrong way.

CHAPTER II

THE USE OF COMPULSION
AND INDUCEMENTS

THE contrasted feelings of what is pleasant or unpleasant are, of course, as definite and directive of canine behaviour as are the rewards and punishments obtained as a result of human conduct. Cakes and the stick, enticement and menace, are expedients used in both cases to induce the desired attitude.

In the matter of compulsion, too, primary and secondary inducements are to be distinguished. With primary compulsive inducements the intermediary is the sense of touch. We are here concerned, in the first place, with mechanical operations, graded from weak to strong, in the form of pulls, pressure, jerks, thrusts and heaves, and in the second place with the infliction of pain, from slight to intense.

Secondary inducements, for effect at a distance, are in the first place accents, ranging from gently admonitory to loudly menacing, words of command, including an intimidating sound such as 'Bah!', and in the second place our bodily attitudes and movements, graded from a threatened to an actual attack upon the dog. These means of compulsion may be used in combination or singly according to circumstances.

Implements to be used in the case of primary compulsive inducements are the collar, the choke collar, and the spiked collar,[1] in combination with the lead. There is also the switch, which can and should be used with a lightning flick of the wrist. Finally, there are the operations at a distance. The difference between the use of the collar and the switch consists in the fact that their mechanical processes are distinct. In conjunction with the lead the collar not only serves to cause discomfort but simultaneously to draw the dog to the trainer's left side. In the down exercises a flick with the switch inflicts discomfort and simultaneously causes the dog to drop down in an instant.

[1] PUBLISHERS' NOTE: The use of the spiked collar, as pointed out by the author in 'heel on lead', is rarely necessary and then only in the case of exceptionally difficult dogs and in the hands of experienced trainers.

Secondary compulsive inducements influence the dog from its youth onward because, as a rule, menacing sounds and movements are immediately followed, or even simultaneously accompanied, by unpleasant consequences. Whether, and if so to what extent, menacing sounds and movements may be regarded as primary inducements must remain an open question.

The next step is a methodical consolidation of the associations formed. It is evident that compulsion may be employed in very different degrees of intensity. The lifting of the paw of a lapdog as a primary inducement to inculcate the giving of the paw is of a compulsive character. So is the gently admonitory sound which serves, for example, to call the dog into the room to feed; while an instance of harsher compulsion is a tug at the collar or a flick with the switch. Even the most soft-hearted dog-owner cannot get on terms with his idolized favourite without some form of compulsion. In the absence of compulsion neither human education nor canine training is feasible.

We now have to decide when to employ minor or major compulsion and the way in which it should be employed. We may first consider the pleasure we may give a dog. It is very easy to satisfy him. As a primary inducement we may make use of fondling, which means stroking and patting the dog and occasionally offering him tit-bits. For work at a distance we introduce secondary inducements, making use, in the course of the fondling, of the encouraging expression 'There's a good boy' and, when necessary, talking to the animal in caressing tones. Even from puppyhood he recognizes such accents as standing in a time relationship to corresponding human action. Systematic use may also be made of primary inducements in the form of movements accompanied by caresses or caressing sounds. These movements include the reduction of the visible area of the body; for example, bending down as well as walking or running backwards away from the dog, as in teaching heel work. (For further details see the Section on the recall.)

We must now consider the application of comfort and discomfort. In the case of human beings who are able to speak we can make them understand why they are punished and rewarded. This cannot be done in the case of the dog. Here we are restricted to the use of external inducements, the reasons for which remain unknown to the animal. It is only through experience of our inducements that the dog can discover where its own advantage or disadvantage lies. We are here concerned with a lesson that, as we shall see, only achieves the object of the training when the experiences under consideration occur *simultaneously*. The first distinction to be made in the application of compulsion is that between *abstention* and *action*, whichever is aimed at. If the former is involved, any natural behaviour on the part of the dog which we may regard as undesirable is suppressed. It is not correct to call this prohibitive training, since the dog neither understands what a prohibition is nor that anything is being prohibited. The same situation obtains here as in the case of a child not yet able to speak which has burnt itself. The child can only learn by experience that fire close at hand is painful. When we are suppressing typical canine conduct, therefore, we should speak of training in abstention.

Hunting game is pleasurable. A dog's inclination to hunt can be suppressed by changing the pleasure into displeasure. This will only occur if the animal learns from experience that it is the actual hunting of game that is attended by unpleasant consequences. For this purpose correction must begin while the dog is hunting, not after he has finished doing so. If the trainer punishes a dog on its return from the chase, the desired association, viz. that hunting is painful, will not be formed, but instead, the thoroughly undesirable one that to approach the trainer after the extreme pleasure of a chase is painful. Since in these circumstances hunting itself remains a pleasure, it is again indulged in by the dog at the first opportunity. If a similar 'punishment' is then repeated, the dog grows more and more afraid to return and becomes hand-shy. The trainer will be wrong to interpret this behaviour as due to a guilty conscience. It has to be constantly borne in mind that the animal can never learn the reason for a disagreeable experience, but only that certain modes of behaviour result in disagreeable experiences.

If a dog is to be prevented from killing a chicken, the correction must be given at the time when the dog has the intention of doing so. Nevertheless, the chicken he has killed can be used as a temporary expedient to stop him doing so again. While the dead bird is held close to the eyes and nose of the animal, he is given a few flicks with the switch, not by way of punishment, but in order to form the association we desire between the scent and view of the chicken and the re-action of fear in its presence provoked by the 'chicken-pain'. It would not occur to anyone whose mind works along anthro-pomorphic lines that such an association might be established successfully by means of a live bird *before* the the dog has ever killed one. For a 'punishment prior to the crime' would, of course, be regarded by such a person as an absurdity.

In the case of all inherited impulses to action, for example the natural, but in the working dog undesirable, association between observing game and pursuing it, it is most important not to give any impetus to the canine inclination in question by any sort of indulgence, since it will then be very difficult to suppress. It must be nipped in the bud before it begins to be active. For this reason compulsion *before* the actual deed must be regarded as an especially urgent measure, it being far easier to prevent a habit being formed than to break off one already formed. It is only possible to break the dog of a habit which we do not desire, while the stimuli which provoke such activity are working on the animal's senses, and if, *at the same time*, he has a disagreeable experience. If the sense-stimuli in question are separated in time and space from the disagreeable experi-ence or 'punishment', it will prove impossible to establish the required association. In such a case the dog will learn an altogether perverted lesson, which the trainer has failed to fore-see. If an infant which had burnt itself only noticed the pain some considerable time after the burning took place, at the moment, say, when it was embracing its mother, the child would learn to fear, not the fire, but its mother. In the same way a dog will learn to fear its trainer rather than the activity concerned, if 'punishment' follows at an interval of time and space in the absence of the sense-stimulus which provoked the undesirable action.

The discontinuance of a particular activity can in many cases be arranged, precisely as in the example 'a burnt child dreads the fire', by causing the disagreeable experience to emanate, not from the trainer, but from the events themselves, in other words from the carriers of the sense-stimuli under observation. For example, certain objects could be placed above a settee, upon which we did not wish a dog to jump, in such a way that the moment he jumped on to it they would come clattering down upon him. Or, again, in order that a dog should not form the habit of running after cyclists, one could arrange for the cyclist himself to give the dog a disagreeable experience. But, as a rule, the trainer himself must be the source of such an experience. Not only is this procedure unattended by disadvantages, *if compulsion is correctly applied*, but it actually facilitates the unconditional submission of the dog to his trainer and guide. In this connection the following point should be carefully noted. The disagreeable experience which emanates from the trainer represents him to the dog *at first* as a bringer of discomfort. The stimulus situation then has to be so arranged that the trainer, in his guise of a bringer of discomfort, retreats into the background and the foreground is occupied by the other stimulus, for example the chicken, with its undesirable reaction on the dog: the impulse to kill, that has to be changed to the reaction we require, i.e. the impulse to leave it alone. In this stimulus-complex of trainer and chicken the chicken must, so to speak, become the pain-bringer to the dog. This position would be impeded if the dog, after receiving a flick from the switch near the chicken, were to suffer any additional discomforts in *isolation* from it, for instance, by being beaten, tied up, locked up, kept without food and abused in threatening accents. By mistakenly extending compulsion the trainer, in his capacity of provider of discomfort, steps into the foreground and consequently gives the dog a permanent fear of him. For in these circumstances the association 'chicken-disagreeable' cannot be established. The disagreeable experience could, of course, be prolonged simply by bringing the chicken under protracted observation by the dog, for example, by tying him up near to a chicken. But in this case the trainer would have to keep a continuous watch so as to be able to apply discomfort immediately the dog showed the slightest interest in the chicken. The trainer should, of course, make no such application so long as the dog remains indifferent to the chicken. Experience of this kind would cause the chicken as pain-bringer to come gradually to occupy the foreground of the dog's attention. The process would, however, be more rapid if the trainer provided agreeable and disagreeable experiences in methodical alternation. Before the dog comes into contact with chickens at all, its trainer might embark at some considerable distance away upon some exercise that pleases the dog. After a while he might take the dog, on the lead, into the neighbourhood of chickens and suddenly give it a disagreeable experience, such as a cut with the switch the moment the dog shows the least interest in them. Thereupon the exercise with agreeable associations would be renewed, and so on. The difference between the first and the second experiment consists in the fact that owing to the frequent alternation of a brief disagreeable experience near the chicken and a longer agreeable one away from it, the bird, with its unpleasant associations, comes more quickly into the foreground and the trainer retreats more quickly into the background.

In the change from the disagreeable to the agreeable experience it should also be arranged that the 'agreeable', with its invariably encouraging effect, does not proceed from the trainer so long as the other stimulus continues to operate upon the dog. If, for example, immediately after a cut with the switch the sound of encouragement is uttered while the dog is still observing the chicken, the mood of encouragement that then begins may easily arouse the dog's inclination to relapse into undesirable behaviour. In all cases where it is only a question of refraining from some action, it is of advantage not to follow the disagreeable with an agreeable experience so long as the object to which the dog is to take a dislike remains under his observation. The depressed mood due to compulsion in these circumstances should not be relieved until further compulsion has been applied.

We may now proceed from training in abstention to training for action. Here it is desired to obtain some sort of action from the dog. We can no more speak of training by giving orders than we can speak of training by issuing prohibitions. It is often not a question of giving orders but permission. If, for example, a dog sees game running away; there is no need for us to order him to follow it. He does so instinctively, of his own accord. We are in luck if, in training a dog, we can use his instincts as a basis for what we require. For the more instinctive an action is the more reliable it will be. Use should, therefore, be made of the dog's instincts wherever it is at all possible. Advice on this point will be given when we come to deal with individual exercises.

It is, however, often only possible to obtain a specific action by means of the external compulsion we have been discussing. This is the case when what is required does not correspond, or only partially corresponds, with a natural action. Instigatory compulsion of this type is then applied as follows. In a mild form of compulsion mechanical inducements are resorted to, though their actual operation obviously does not remain purely mechanical, for the accompanying sense-stimuli are transmitted to the brain and grasped by the memory. If, for example, a dog is to be trained to offer its paw, we lift up its paw in order to achieve our object, thus ourselves performing the movement the dog is to learn. Simultaneously with this primary inducement we make use of a secondary one, by uttering, for instance, the words 'Give your paw'.

If the action required from the dog is associated with a bodily activity, the corresponding physical movement has, as a rule, to be performed by the trainer himself in the prescribed mechanical fashion, until the dog has learnt his lesson. This mechanical compulsion is in many cases insufficient, as when highly unnatural behaviour is required. Additional measures must then be taken as a powerful form of compulsion. This involves the infliction of some degree of pain. The anthropomorphic type of mind often falls into the error of supposing that with the novice dog pain *only* is necessary, without the application of the mechanical impulse which is equally essential for promoting activity.

If the dog has to be compelled to pick up and fetch an object disagreeable to him, a mechanical inducement will bring about this performance with astonishing rapidity, causing the dog, under the infliction of pain, to dash with lightning speed to the object and at the same time to open his jaws. In the case of the novice dog, therefore, whenever an action is to be obtained under a powerful form of compulsion, two forces combine to complete the operation, the mechanical impulse responsible for the physical movement in question and the simultaneous stimulation by discomfort. How does the dog, in such a case, learn that the act required is to his own advantage?

THE THEORY OF TRAINING

He does so by virtue of the fact that the compulsion, i.e. either the mechanical impulse alone or the same impulse combined with discomfort, ceases the moment the act required by the trainer begins. Thus, in giving the paw, as soon as the paw reaches the position required, or in retrieving, as soon as the object to be fetched is grasped, all compulsion stops.

With a powerful form of compulsion we must also ensure that the initial discomfort subsequently turns into pleasure. We have no wish to see a panic-stricken slave doing what we want in fear and trembling, but a dog that enjoys life and is happy in his work, putting all his heart into it. Just as the art of human education is to substitute desire for obligation, that of animal training requires a disagreeable activity to be changed into an agreeable one. This aim is achieved, in the first place, by the *limitation of compulsion* already prescribed: it must stop the very instant the act required begins. Secondly, it is essential that as soon as the disagreeable experience ceases, an agreeable one follows immediately, as a regular consequence. The result of this liberation from the pressure of compulsion is that the dog quickly learns how to escape from his disagreeable experience and, in addition, finds that the act, though in itself disagreeable, is soon transformed into an agreeable experience. This causes him to develop an amazing zest for his work. The anthropomorphic view, which demands, not from the infant, but, strangely enough, from the dog, 'conscious obedience and conscious performance of duty' and gives a false interpretation to the act carried out by a dog under compulsion, is responsible for the fact that too little use is made of the principle that an agreeable experience should be provided after the execution of any act required. In utter ignorance of what is required to get on terms with the animal, such a trainer will stand as stiff as a ramrod, with uplifted forefinger and the menacing attitude of a schoolmaster, to see that his orders are carried out. This is the reason for the existence of so many panic-stricken dogs that take no pleasure in their work.

The agreeable experience that follows compulsion enables the dog quickly to recognize where his advantage lies. In providing it the trainer will find his best chance to give rein to the most exuberant expression of the warmth of his feelings. He ought, as soon as the required act is performed and also when

C

even the slightest progress is apparent, not only to utter such words as 'good boy' repeatedly in caressing tones, and fondle the dog, but also, if the exercise in hand permits it, to execute a dance of joy with the animal. What the trainer actually says on such occasions, as distinct from the auditory and visual signals, which would always remain the same, is a matter of indifference. In such a case the caressing accents and corresponding gestures of the trainer supply all the 'music' necessary. The effect of the pulling and pushing movements made by the trainer is also almost wholly ignored by most people. All the physical movements which excite a dog's instinct to play are capable of arousing the utmost delight in him.

We may now recapitulate. The chief differences between training a dog to abstain and training him for activity under external compulsion are as follows. In the former case natural modes of behaviour are suppressed by giving the dog a disagreeable experience. A certain type of action is thus rendered obnoxious to the dog.

In activity-training associated with external compulsion, on the other hand, the dog is impelled to perform unnatural and often uncongenial actions by mechanical inducements, sometimes accompanied by temporary discomfort. The performance of the required action is rendered agreeable to the dog by the use of caressing accents and fondling as soon as it has been executed.

There are a number of exercises which comprise simultaneous training in activity and abstention. For example, the down begins with an act, that of lying down, but ends with abstention, the refraining from getting up. In such cases compulsion, as in abstention training proper, would not achieve its object by taking the form of encouragement, if the required abstention is one which contrasts strongly with any natural canine attitude, as happens, for instance, in the case of a dog dismissed and left to itself.

Other exercises are mainly concerned with action. For example, in heel on lead it is principally an act, that of following at the left side of the trainer, which is required. But an abstention is also involved: the dog must not leave the trainer's side. In such cases the compulsive inducement to abstain should at once be followed by encouragement as soon as the very slightest

THE THEORY OF TRAINING

response by the dog is noticed. (Further details will be found in Chapter III together with instructions on the treatment of all individual exercises, especially that of the recall.) No account is taken, in considering the mode of application of compulsion, of scent discrimination (training to pattern).

Erroneous application of compulsion is a deeply rooted evil in training. It is a common practice for such 'punishments' as are utterly opposed to the object in view to be brought into operation in relation to the recall, by a mistaken extension of the compulsion principle. This gives rise to hand-shyness and a general state of terror in the dog, leading to the false conclusion that a trainer should not venture to inflict any but mild compulsion during training.

In the first place, too mild compulsion may render a dog unreliable in a number of exercises when the real services of a working dog are required. In many cases the dog will only work when he happens to be in the mood. In the second place, if only mild compulsion is used, a dog may very easily defy the trainer. In a pack of young dogs fierce fights take place to decide how they are to rank within the pack. And in a pack composed of men and dogs, canine competition for importance in the eyes of the trainer is keen. If this state of affairs is not countered by methods which the canine mind can comprehend, it frequently ends in such animals attacking and seriously injuring not only their trainers, but also other people. As in a pack of dogs, the order of hierarchy in a man and dog combination can only be established by physical force, that is by an actual struggle, in which the man is instantly victorious. Such a result can only be brought about by convincing the dog of the absolute physical superiority of the man. Otherwise the dog will lead and the man follow. If a dog shows the slightest sign of rebellion against his trainer or leader, the physical superiority of the man as leader of the pack must be given instant expression in the most unmistakable manner.

Should a dog rebel against his trainer, instant resort to severe compulsion is essential. The dog must, of course, be on the lead at the time, to prevent his defence turning to attack. For, each time the dog finds that he is not instantly mastered, the canine competitive instinct will increase and his submissive instinct will weaken. One of the objects of training, however, is to inculcate the reverse condition. It is not, of course, so in the case of a lapdog, whose 'naughtiness' may be amusing, but it is invariably so when we are concerned with a dog that may attack his trainer and become dangerous, or with a dog in the public service.

If a dog that resists his trainer is not on the lead at the time, the exercise that gave rise to the resistance must be at once broken off and the trainer, by running from the dog and at the same time calling him to follow, with a friendly 'That's a good boy', should summon him to heel and receive him with caresses, as if nothing had happened. In order to avoid the formation of an undesirable association, the next step is to allow a certain time to elapse during which the man again fondles the dog at intervals. The same exercise which had initiated the dog's resistance is then proceeded with, at a different place and with the dog on the lead. The animal is thereby challenged to repeat his resistance in order that the trainer may have an opportunity to settle the question of precedence of authority in the only way he can. For example, in the exceptional case in which the dog snarls at the trainer and a heavy cut with the switch does not stop him, a beating must follow. Such treatment will in such a case stimulate the submissive instinct, without weakening the pack impulse—loyalty and readiness to come to heel. Such weakening will only occur if, as already repeatedly stated, punishment is applied in conjunction with coming to heel.

The switch should be employed until the animal submits and his will to resist, and the exasperation that accompanies it, is replaced by fear. So long as the dog does not submit, but continues to resist, a flexible switch should be used, if necessary, on the head and jaws, but not on the top of the nose. It may also be used on the neck, ears, legs and tail, but not on the sexual parts or on the lower regions of the belly and chest. Apart from such exceptional cases *heavy* cuts should only be applied to the powerful muscles on the fore- and hindquarters and on the back.[1]

Certain tough types of dog will refuse to give in despite the

---

[1] PUBLISHERS' NOTE: It should be remembered that the author is referring to Service dogs, many of which are savage and if not kept under control could endanger the life of the handler.

most energetic counter-action by the trainer. Such animals are unsuitable for training as working dogs.

The form of compulsion just described differs from that of which an account was previously given in that it does not involve instruction by association-forming, properly so called. We are concerned here with a struggle for authority. The object of compulsion is to obtain the permanent and unconditional surrender of the dog. The intimidated state that accompanies it soon disappears, simply because peace again reigns as soon as the man is victorious.

Individual dogs differ widely both physically and psychologically. For that reason methods of treatment must also vary, not only as between dogs of different breeds, but also between those of the same breed.

The extent to which physical demands can be made on a dog without injuring him depends on his age and on his build. The present work is mainly concerned with the training of dogs which are mature, or very nearly so. In the section dealing with individual exercises, cases are indicated in which especial care should be taken to avoid making excessive physical demands on the animal.

Variations in character may be inherited or acquired during the individual dog's life. There may be hereditary differences in keenness of the senses and powers of understanding (mental), as well as in instinct and feeling (emotional). Variation in capacity for service is the result of one of these powers predominating over the other. A high level of keenness of the senses and a good faculty of understanding do not necessarily guarantee good service. This capacity also involves, as among men, the power of the will, which is dependent upon instinctive and emotional life.

The instincts of the domestic dog, for instance, the instinct for freedom, the defensive instinct, that of the pack and that of the chase, are not always developed in the same degree in individual animals. This necessitates differences in the disciplinary methods employed, according to the object in view. For example, a pronounced instinct of the chase is desirable in a hunting dog, but not in a working dog. Variation in instinct may be caused by the absence of the struggle for existence, whereby natural selection is impeded. In a state of nature defective instincts, such as a defective instinct of flight from impending danger, may be punished with death. There are some instincts which we do not consider desirable in a domestic dog, for example, that of flight just mentioned. If this were very pronounced it would have a prejudicial effect upon loyalty. We do not, therefore, in breeding our dogs, follow nature in every respect. The kind of artificial selection we make in breeding causes considerable variation in the condition and strength of instincts. It is the same in the sphere of the emotions. We have dogs of weak character with great sensitivity to unpleasant experiences and dogs of strong character with less sensitivity. We also have temperamental differences. There are, too, differences resulting from propensities acquired during life, that is those formed as a result of the individual animal's experiences.

The inherited and acquired diversities mentioned become very apparent under training. Thus the number of repetitions requisite for learning a particular exercise vary. The larger the number of repetitions necessary the longer will be the period of training under compulsion. This circumstance does not affect the principles of the application of compulsion. Different degrees of compulsion have to be applied to individual animals. A dog possessing highly developed sexual and hunting instincts and a less pronounced pack instinct will, for example, call for stricter compulsion in bringing it to heel than will an animal in which the pack instinct is pronounced but the other two less developed.

Different degrees of compulsion have, moreover, to be applied to dogs of strong and weak character. In the case of the latter a sound uttered in a threatening tone is often sufficient to cause the desired action to be carried out, while the same result can only be obtained with a tough or very lively dog by the infliction of some degree of pain.

In this connection it should be stressed that the number of repetitions does not depend exclusively on the 'cleverness' or 'stupidity' of an individual dog, but that the condition and the strength of the animal's instincts also affect the situation. A 'clever' dog, for instance, with strong instincts, may need a longer period to learn to perform an exercise, if the exercise is not in harmony with the instincts in question, than will a 'stupid' dog with weak instincts.

It must be emphasized, too, that strict compulsion must be applied with special caution to a dog affected by fear. The severer forms of compulsion are, in general, only necessary when reliable and continuous services are required to be performed during the serious, variable and manifold interruptions which may occur on active duty.

Finally, the following considerations should be taken into account in the study of compulsion. Training should take place from the beginning, not in a so-called training-room, but in open country, at different and frequently changed places. In a training-room a dog remains permanently in a state of intimidation because while there he is continually reminded of the compulsion he has undergone in that place in the past. The effect of such recollection is that the moment the dog enters the place he becomes apprehensive. His ability to learn is thus prejudiced and he can take no pleasure in the work. In open country, on the other hand, recollection of compulsion undergone in the past is impeded by the change of locality.

Training indoors is also disadvantageous for another reason: i.e. that no distraction can be encountered. In many exercises, however, distractions render important assistance from the very start. They provoke the dog, at the commencement of his activities, to do something we do not desire. We thus obtain the opportunity, at the outset, to induce him to drop the activity. It is, of course, possible to undertake in a room, without detriment, exercises which have agreeable associations for the dog, such as the rudiments of fetching in play, where distractions are undesirable.

When the dog first starts to learn, only a mild form of compulsion should ever be employed, so as to avoid intimidation and to accustom him, so to speak, to whatever routine behaviour it is desired to impose upon him. If then, as training proceeds, stricter compulsion becomes necessary, the dog is already familiar with the routine and can thus much more readily evade the stricter compulsion than would be the case had it been applied at the outset. When strict compulsion is being used it may not be possible wholly to avoid intimidation. It should, however, be transitory, for strict compulsion must be relaxed or stopped altogether as soon as the object the trainer has in view is achieved.

In order to dispense with intimidation so far as possible it is important to vary the exercises from the very first day. The programme drawn up for the training of working dogs shows what exercises may be undertaken independently of one another from the first day on. An exercise associated with a highly disagreeable experience is followed by one which will be wholly agreeable to the animal. Each separate exercise that brings about the desired behaviour on the part of the dog should end with fondling.

Until training in the down and coming to heel exercises have rendered the dog submissive, work should only proceed while he is on the lead. In any case, special care should be taken to prevent the dog being able, even on a single occasion, to escape compulsion by flight. Otherwise the instinct of flight, so disadvantageous for training, will be fostered.

Before leaving this subject we may refer to an important point regarding the psychological attitude of the trainer in applying compulsion. Many people are still apt to think in terms of rewards and punishments, praise and blame. This idea prevents the abrupt change which is so necessary between the provision of disagreeable and agreeable experiences. The latter lesson is the first which the trainer has to learn. It is most important that the novice trainer should be very careful how he tackles the question of compulsion. This is the chief reason why it is advisable, in all exercises, always to start with only a mild form of compulsion. The experienced trainer, who has already learnt how to manage the abrupt change from agreeable to disagreeable in a workmanlike manner, can, in many cases, as in training in heel work, ignore this rule and apply a strict form of compulsion without delay. The dog is so amenable to discipline that when the *appropriate* measures are taken to come to an understanding with him, he learns very quickly what is to his advantage or disadvantage.

To return to the subject of memory, when it is desired to memorize anything we can, as a rule, only do so, as already pointed out, by repetition. But it is possible for a unique event to be retained by the memory for a considerable time or even permanently. This is the case with both men and dogs and applies to either very disagreeable or very agreeable occurrences. A bomb may burst with a loud noise and at the same time so seriously wound a dog carrying despatches that great pain is felt. Auditory stimulus and pain at once establish the association expressed by the phrase, 'the sound of a bursting bomb hurts'. If a conspicuous visual stimulus, for example a single tree, happens to be present at the spot where the wounding takes place, this object may also participate in the association as a pain-bringer. The dog would thereafter experience fear in the presence not only of bursting bombs but of single trees. Such an association might well last a lifetime. It may be incidentally observed that this type of association would not be formed if, as often happens, the pain of the wound were not instantly felt.

On the other hand, events which do not powerfully excite the animal do not cause the formation of an association for any considerable time. Here compulsion lends artificial aid. *Properly applied* strict compulsion produces the desired association more quickly than frequent mild compulsion.

The number of repetitions required cannot be stated. It will depend, as already mentioned, on the psychological type of the individual dog, on the extent to which the service demanded is natural or unnatural to it and also on the skill of the trainer. Neither with men nor dogs is a lesson always retained permanently in the memory. We forget, for instance, a telephone number which we have memorized unless we repeat it from time to time. Practice is requisite in order to remember a lesson. It may be mentioned here that we have an advantage over the dog in memorization because we have the wish to learn our lesson and this enables us to learn more quickly than if we had no such desire. The dog never has any desire to learn and has no idea what our object is in making use of him. There is a second point in which the dog falls short of us. We often find it wearisome to learn things by heart and try to render the process less exhausting. In order to improve our memories we introduce artificial aids. It is easier to remember the number of days in each month if we memorize the old rhyme 'Thirty days hath September . . .' and so on.

To the question whether continual application of secondary inducements alone will enable the dog always to remember what he has learnt, the answer must be in the negative. We shall not be able to make the dog instantly lie down by always employing the auditory signal 'Down!' alone, nor cause him to come to heel when he is in the open and in the presence of strong distractions by always employing the auditory signal 'Here!' alone. The trainer must, therefore, from time to time reform the associations, in other words resort to the primary inducements while simultaneously using the secondary ones, just as he did during the original lessons. This expedient is especially necessary in the case of exercises running counter to the nature of the animal.

From this it will be seen how mistaken it is to say that a dog has now learnt how to perform this or that service and knows what his duty is. If a child is unable, one day, to repeat a poem which it has learnt by heart some considerable time ago, it will be impossible to force what has been forgotten into its memory by any kind of punishment. The only action we can take is to renew repetition of the poem. Yet how often a dog is 'punished' when one day he fails to perform an exercise he has satisfactorily performed in the past! Apart from lack of practice the cause in such cases may be that some fresh distraction, to which the dog is not yet accustomed, has occurred. It is useless to resort to blows in such a case. Instead of shouting and cursing, the trainer must, as already stated, resort to the primary inducements and recognize that in so doing he is merely carrying out a necessary part of training.

Apart from continual practice, it is also essential, for the retention of associations, to undertake the successive parts of the series of exercises appropriate to active service in the same order, so far as possible from the very start of instruction. No part should ever be omitted, otherwise the associations will weaken and finally disappear. For instance, if the dog acting as escort is required (a) to search a stretch of country, (b) to bark at every human being found in it and fetch back every object that has the scent of humanity about it and (c) to seize and detain anyone found who tries to get away, and on several occasions the dog makes the search without finding anyone, thus failing to carry out (b) and (c), the associations established will be gradually weakened. Moreover, the dog will lose interest in the work, because the events that would excite the animal, namely the discovery of objects and persons, do not occur.

We have mentioned that the ultimate aim of training is to

be able to control the dog simply by means of secondary inducements, that is by making auditory and visual signals. In training to this end the secondary inducements must be steadily toned down, the auditory signals more and more softly uttered, and slighter and slighter bodily movements employed for the visual signals, since the dog has to learn to do his duty on receipt of the lightest possible stimulus. This requirement is frequently essential on active service, especially where work has to be carried out with the dog as silently as possible.

The trainer should adopt a natural and easy-going attitude towards the dog. If he attains to the necessary knowledge of the nature of canine aptitudes he will be able to increase their quality and steadiness, while the animal will benefit by the mild nature of a system of training which is based upon an appreciation of canine mentality.

Part II

PRACTICAL TRAINING

CHAPTER III

ACTION AND ABSTENTION—ACCELERATION OF PACE—DISCIPLINARY EXERCISES

I. ACTION AND ABSTENTION

SOUND of encouragement: 'There's a good boy' (loud, caressing and long-drawn-out tone).

Intimidating sound: 'Bah!' (deep-voiced, threatening and brief).

Agreeable and disagreeable experiences are the reins whereby we guide the dog and make him understand where his advantage or disadvantage lies.

It is of decisive importance for training to be able to provide agreeable and disagreeable experiences at a distance. Primary compulsive inducements are the reins that work directly upon the body; they are, therefore, in the main, employed only when the dog is on the lead or in our immediate neighbourhood. The psychological reins with which we are able to guide the dog at a distance are furnished by the secondary inducements of auditory and visual signals. According to the tone of voice in uttering the auditory signals and the type of gesture made, the agreeable or disagreeable experience can be provoked. Special auditory signals, namely encouraging and intimidating sounds, also serve this purpose. Though these secondary inducements may not be so effective as the primary, they do in many cases provoke the desired behaviour.

A certain sound should be made to form an association with agreeable experience by accompanying every fondling or caress administered to the dog with such words as 'There's a good boy'. Another sound is made to form an association with disagreeable experience. Whenever such an experience is given to the dog, the sound 'Bah!' is made, for instance with the slap administered when the dog begs at table, or when the lead is jerked if the dog attempts to chase a cat while on the lead. Such cases do not include those in which a sound other than 'Bah!' is requisite for the exercise in question. For example, in the down exercise mechanical compulsion is accompanied by the sound 'Down' and in teaching heel work the word 'Heel' is uttered when the dog is pulled in.

It should be clearly understood that sounds of encouragement and intimidation only become effective when regularly repeated simultaneously with the primary inducements.

The proper employment of the two sounds is considerably facilitated for the trainer if he regards them simply as promoters of an agreeable or disagreeable experience, and consequently of encouragement or intimidation, not as expressions of praise or blame.

In the carrying out of any action a distinction must be made between a refusal to undertake such action and its suspension. If the dog refuses to carry out a certain action, for example, the picking up of metal, the auditory signal appropriate to the exercise, in this case 'Fetch it', is uttered in a threatening tone, if necessary in combination with a form of strict compulsion. The moment the required action begins the phrase 'There's a good boy' is spoken and repeated several times during the performance of the service. On the other hand, if an action required and already in progress is broken off, e.g. when in tracking a dog sniffs at a mouse-hole, we may employ one or more of the 'Bah!' sounds, followed by repetition of the phrase 'There's a good boy' directly the compulsion has the desired effect.

If it is only the discontinuance of an action that is desired, without being directly followed by another action required by the trainer, the 'Bah!' is not succeeded by 'There's a good boy'. The dog may be barking in its kennel or begging at table. In such cases liberation from the intimidation imposed by the 'Bah!' is unnecessary and even undesirable, since the encouragement promoted by the phrase 'There's a good boy' may easily cause the dog to return to the action which had to be broken off.

We must watch carefully the gestures with which we accompany agreeable and disagreeable experiences. If such movements are regularly made in conjunction with the auditory signals, the reinforcement thus obtained produces a greater effect than if sounds alone are used. It is much easier to get on terms with a dog if we learn to alternate agreeable and disagreeable experiences with extreme rapidity (see 'Recall' Section).

Fox Photos Ltd.

Alsatian scaling a jump of 9 ft.

C. M. Cooke

Working Collie at heel free

Howard Evans

Alsatian retrieving a Service revolver, a very uncongenial
object, over a gorse hedge

C. M. Cooke

Retrieving in water

Disagreeable experiences should be entirely restricted to critical moments. At other times agreeable experiences should be the rule.

2. ACCELERATION OF PACE

Word of command: 'Get on'.

In certain cases it is important to be able to accelerate a dog's pace without affecting the direction already taken by the animal.

This is particularly desirable in reconnaissance by the guard dog. On active service the animal will often seek for a long time without finding. It is then necessary to force him on occasionally by inciting him with shouts. There must be no snapping of the psychological reins controlling him.

The command 'At him' used in reconnaissance itself, and the accompanying signals, do, of course, incite, but their employment during the work entails the followng disadvantage. If the handler cannot see the dog owing to the lie of the land or darkness, he may call 'At him' at the very moment that the dog is running back to him with an object it has found in its jaws. The signal then turns the dog away from his handler again, since it has become associated with such behaviour in accordance with the primary inducements. Fetching of an object may thus be rendered impracticable for the dog.

The use of an auditory signal that has the effect previously mentioned is necessary, but the dog's direction must not be affected by this sound. The condition will be fulfilled if the phrase 'get on' is only used on the following occasions:

(a) *To induce running ahead:*

(1) When loose and ahead of the trainer.

(2) When the trainer, during performance of the zig-zag method of reconnaissance, or during reconnaissance of lost objects, himself takes a lateral direction, right or left.

(3) When, in going upstairs, a light blow with the switch is surreptitiously given to the dog in front of one. (On arrival at top of stairs one should not forget to liberate the dog from the pressure of this compulsive action.) At a later stage a clattering noise made behind the dog will suffice as a secondary inducement.

D

(*b*) *To induce running to meet the trainer:*

When, during recall training, the trainer runs away from the dog.

If these exercises are practised regularly, the secondary inducement of 'Get on' soon becomes effective when used alone.

3. DISCIPLINARY EXERCISES

(*a*) *Heel on lead.*

Service requirement: When the lead is held loosely the dog is to follow its master at his left side, in such a way that the lead is not drawn tight and remains in the same condition whether the man slackens or puts on speed, turns right or left or about turns. The chest of the moving dog should be practically in line with the left knee of its trainer, so that the latter may keep the animal constantly in view.

Heel on lead can only be taught to dogs already accustomed to a lead and no longer rebellious to its control. A dog on the lead is deprived of its freedom. A barrier has to be placed, by means of compulsion, against the animal's instinct for freedom. We are aided in this task by the submissive and pack instincts. The latter attaches the dog psychologically to human beings and appears in the loyalty he shows, which is so useful to us. We are also aided by the readiness of the dog to learn.

If a dog has not previously been on the lead it will do a great deal of harm to take him out on a short lead, especially with a spiked collar, and drag him along. The dog, thus deprived for the first time of his freedom and also suffering considerable pain, gets into such a state of fear and distraction that it becomes extremely difficult to teach him anything.

The dog should have no distressing experiences when he is being accustomed to the lead. While the lead is being adjusted the sound of encouragement should always be repeated several times, and immediately it has been adjusted the dog's head should be repeatedly stroked or lightly scratched. One should also avoid inflicting disagreeable experiences immediately after adjusting the lead, e.g. no exercises involving compulsion should be undertaken directly afterwards. Nor should the dog ever be struck with the lead. Dogs which have been treated in the proper manner will, after a short time, thrust their heads against the trainer while the lead is being adjusted.

A dog may be accustomed to the lead by being allowed to run loose with a very long lead fastened to his collar. One may hold the other end of the lead and follow the dog but without ever pulling him in. This action should be avoided as far as possible, to prevent the dog from developing hardness of the neck. Should there be an occasional tightening of the lead a gentle jerk is all that is necessary. If the dog should then turn to look at the trainer, which action, apart from any jerk at the lead, may occur if the latter clicks his tongue or slaps his knee, the trainer may drop the lead and run backwards, away from the dog, but keeping the face turned towards him (primary inducement to recall) and repeatedly uttering the sounds of encouragement. When the dog comes up it should be fondled and instantly let loose again. Our first task is to accustom the animal to the lead by means of a weak form of compulsion. Pains should be taken, from the start, not to arouse fear in the dog while he is on the lead.

Heel on lead should not be taught until the dog has become used to the lead.

As already stated, attachment to the lead represents a deprivation of freedom. The dog would much rather be at liberty, near the trainer, to follow its own inclinations. Close attendance at the left side of the trainer has, therefore, to be turned from an unpleasant to a pleasant situation. For this purpose two different inducements are required, according to whether the dog leaves its place at the left side of the trainer in consequence of intimidation or out of high spirits. Many dogs, in spite of previous familiarization with the lead, become frightened when heel work exercises begin. The most unsuitable method that can be used to eradicate fear is a *strict* form of compulsion. In teaching heel work, therefore, one should not drag a frightened animal behind one or even, as is often advised, use the spiked collar to do so. Such measures only serve to increase fear and cause the dog to intensify his efforts to escape and keep behind the trainer. Even forward pulling by the animal would only have the same prejudicial result. In the end a dog handled in this way would become so terrified that he would be useless for other exercises, for instance fetching in play, for some time.

When fear or intimidation have to be dealt with, the remedy is encouragement. It can be applied by frequent fondling of the dog with the left hand, which is free from the lead, while the walk is in progress. Or the trainer can drop to the ground and play with the dog or begin to run, a procedure which usually pleases the animal, meanwhile repeatedly uttering the sound of encouragement as loudly as possible. One can then slow down, when the dog seems ready to do so, and again caress the animal with the left hand. It does no harm at first for the dog to play with the left hand and for that hand to encourage such play. The dog must feel that he is always well looked after when at the man's left side.

Another inducement associated with a mild form of compulsion comes into force when one turns round to the dog, if it lingers, and, while standing still, strikes one's hip with the left hand meanwhile gently pulling the animal in to the left side and uttering the word 'Heel' in a friendly tone. But the lead must always be loosened again as soon as the animal is in the correct position and a caressing 'Heel' must always be uttered, followed by the phrase 'There's a good boy' several times repeated and accompanied by fondling. It is important to loosen the lead immediately after a jerk or pull, to avoid making the dog accustomed to walking on a tight lead. If the animal goes to the right side of its master, he must immediately be drawn to the left with a gently uttered 'Heel', this word being given a progressively more threatening sound as training proceeds. Stricter compulsion should not be commenced until the dog has lost its fear. The animal must feel that to abandon its position at the trainer's left side causes more discomfort than to stay there.

If the dog remains at a distance in front, sideways or behind, out of sheer high spirits, the form of compulsion described below must be applied at the same moment, on each occasion. But it should cease at once as soon as the animal takes up the desired position. He will then regard the place in question as a safe refuge.

We may now consider the appropriate management of the lead.

The left hand grasps the lead in such a way that the dog is brought into the desired attitude, with its chest almost exactly in line with the left knee of the trainer (*see* Fig. 1). The right hand also holds the lead. In this way, if the animal bounds forward, he can be pulled back with the right hand, while the lead is allowed to slip through the left hand. By grasping the lead with the right hand the left hand is left free and can be used to attract the dog to one's side by caressing gestures.

FIG. 1
Heel on lead

FIG. 2
Heel on lead

During training the trainer should continually give the dog fresh opportunities to leave his left side, so that he may apply the necessary correction. This procedure would be impossible if the lead were always kept so short as to prevent the animal from moving forward, sideways or backwards. It is necessary for him to leave his position and to experience discomfort as a result, and for this purpose, as already emphasized, regular loosening of the lead is essential (*see* Fig. 2).

The following are the primary inducements:

1. *To counter bounding forward, when due to high spirits:* the jerking back of the dog with the lead, abrupt turns, while still walking, to the left, so that the dog collides with the trainer's left knee; walking leftwards in a circle; walking leftwards round a narrow tree-trunk or post, while keeping close to it; walking

up to a narrow tree-trunk and making a sudden turn to the right when almost touching it. A flick with the switch may be added if necessary when training is fairly far advanced.

2. *To counter remaining at a distance, sideways:* drawing or pulling in with the lead; walking up to a narrow tree-trunk and passing close to it (i.e. without turning); this often causes the dog to collide with the tree, or, if he passes the tree on the left, he can be pulled in by the trainer.

3. *To counter remaining at a distance, when this does not occur as the result of intimidation, but of distraction, as when the animal sniffs at the ground, looks round at his hindquarters and so on:* the left arm is stretched out and the right hand draws or pulls the lead, so that the dog is pulled in. Turning or walking in a circle to the right, simultaneously pulling at the lead, may also be resorted to.

During all these inducements the word 'Heel' is uttered and the lead immediately loosened as soon as the dog comes to the trainer's left side. After the 'Heel' a caressing 'There's a good boy' is repeatedly uttered when the animal takes up the proper position. The accent with which the word 'Heel' is pronounced will differ according to whether it is desired to encourage or intimidate.

Walking should begin slowly but should soon achieve a good round pace, and thereafter there should be sudden changes of speed in the walk. Abrupt halts and running about with the lead may also be practised, as well as walking and running straight ahead.

The trainer should know that the severity of the compulsion to be applied must be governed by the aptitude shown by the individual dog. He should always employ encouragement when working with timid dogs.

Search may be made for distractions right from the very first day. They are the best means of enabling the requisite primary inducements to be used, the dog on the lead being always under the direct control of the trainer. As training goes on, strong distractions should be deliberately sought out; heel work, for example, should be practised in the presence of other dogs as well as when in sight of a 'criminal' and before and after manwork. These measures afford the best opportunity for the employment of strong compulsion.

Though the secondary inducement 'Heel' becomes effective in the course of training when used alone, it must nevertheless be frequently reinforced by the simultaneous use of primary inducements, for the behaviour required from the dog is contrary to its nature.

The trainer should also be warned against certain undesirable associations which may easily be formed during practice. The down and standing still exercises should not be performed immediately before or immediately after training in heel on lead or heel free. The primary inducements which have to be employed in such exercises make the dog timid and if he finds that the uncongenial exercises of 'Down' and standing still are associated with heel work, he will experience fear during practice of the latter.

If, exceptionally, after adjustment of the lead any exercises involving compulsion are undertaken, one should always bestow caresses while the lead is being attached to the collar. One has to force oneself to do this because treatment associated with compulsion often encounters resistance by the dog. This resistance may have annoyed the trainer and he may feel very far from being in the mood to associate adjustment of the lead with a caress. On such occasions the rule is to allow an interval to elapse before undertaking the compulsion exercise.

Finally, there remains to be discussed the question whether heel on lead is to be taken to mean that the dog is never to put his nose to the ground, nor to look, listen or take up a scent right or left, but to keep his attention fixed almost exclusively on the movements of his master and not trouble himself about stimuli in his environment. Every trainer knows that a dog which is submissive to the lead on ordinary walks is not usually so on active service. That sounds as though the dog were aware of the difference between the two situations, but, of course, that is not the case. The fact is that the animal remains submissive on ordinary exercise because his master's turning movements, which then usually begin at once, instantly remind him of the corrective instruction he has had in the past; such movements do not often occur on active service, when long distances are covered without turning round. The consequence is that heel work has to be practised with particular care when working on duty.

No one is likely to maintain that it is advantageous for the dog's master if the animal accompanying him on serious work takes no notice of stimuli in the environment. On the contrary, it is precisely the use of the dog's keen senses that helps man at such times. The technique of training an escorting animal is actually directed to developing the attention of the dog to human beings and scents, so that he may be able to give his handler important information. It has to be admitted, of course, that the dog may occasionally notify its master of something, for instance, a cat, peculiarly calculated to appeal to the animal's instincts, which can never be entirely suppressed. Such behaviour should not be discouraged when it is merely the dog's attention that has been aroused. But if the instinct of the chase begins to operate in the animal, it must be counteracted.

During those exercises, involving stimuli for the dog which differ from those of active service, the best method to adopt in training is to make the dog follow without paying attention to anything else, with his head permanently up, the reason being that the compulsion then involved will more effectively promote the dog's submission.

In conclusion, we may refer to the matter of the spiked collar. In teaching heel work the trainer has at his disposal sufficient powerful compulsive inducements without resorting to the use of the spiked collar. He can, for instance, cause the dog, when it bounds forward, to collide with the trainer's knee, or, when it remains at a distance, cause it to bump into a tree and so on, so that with the average dog the spiked collar is superfluous. It is never necessary in the case of tough types of dog which have not been spoiled by bad training and if used at all should be applied only in exceptional cases where a particularly refractory animal has to be broken of an undesirable habit.

(b) *Behaviour off the lead.*
    (i) *Heel free.*
Auditory signal: 'Heel'.

The dog has already learnt to escape the menace of danger notified to him by the sound 'Heel' by rapidly coming close to the trainer.

The foundations of the first attempts to make the dog follow its master when off the lead have also been laid in heel on lead. During the latter the dog may be released but attached to the lead again and subjected to still stricter inducement the moment difficulties are encountered in making him follow. A fresh attempt to make him do so is then inaugurated.

The demands made on him are only gradually increased. The abrupt turns made during lead practice may also be used when the dog is off the lead but not, at first, when it bounds forward. Movement round trees is never undertaken. One should be satisfied, to begin with, with walking straight ahead and making very slight turns. In contrast with practice on the lead, distractions should in the early stages be avoided and only looked for when the dog has become submissive in the released state. Compulsion at the start, as in heel on lead, should only take a mild form.

Dogs which remain behind as a consequence of distractions are called to order by a sharply uttered 'Heel!', instantly followed by the encouragement sound, the trainer himself breaking into a run. If this expedient does not work, strict compulsion must immediately be employed again, for which purpose the dog must be attached to the lead, with fondling gestures as before.

Particular care should be taken in using compulsion upon timid dogs that tend to remain behind. Encouragement is the most suitable method to employ in such cases. Running by the trainer (see Heel on Lead) will have an extremely encouraging effect. In so doing the trainer strikes his hip with his left hand and when the dog returns to his side strokes it and utters the words 'Heel—there's a good boy' in a caressing tone.

If the dog should ever come to the trainer's right side, the latter should stand still and with the right hand (never with the left) give the animal a light slap. Directly afterwards the left side should be turned to the dog and it should be attracted with the left hand, as described in Heel on Lead, to the left side, or else the trainer should break into a run directly after giving the slap.

When first released from the lead the dog will probably remain behind or bound forward to a considerable distance. On

the first occasion it is an excellent plan for the trainer to begin
to run. If the dog has bounded off some way ahead, the trainer
should turn round immediately and walk or run in a straight
line away from the animal. If the dog strays to a considerable
distance, the caressingly uttered word 'Here' may be used
(instead of 'Heel') and the primary inducements to recall
employed.

(ii) *Ahead of Trainer*.
Auditory signal: 'Get on'.
The dog should not be allowed to remain permanently at
heel. A dog belonging to a private owner will, of course, be
permitted to enjoy the freedom of release from the lead more
regularly than a working dog. But the latter, too, should from
time to time be given the opportunity to be at liberty, especially during training, when he is subjected to such drastic
compulsion.

Release of the trained working dog from the lead must not,
however, take up much of his time. Otherwise he may easily
get accustomed to pursuing undesirable inclinations. Heel work,
too, will be greatly prejudiced, for the dog, in anticipation of
being let loose, will be always straining ahead.

The trainer may be walking straight on with the released
dog following at his heels. Suddenly he will run a few steps
forward, associating this primary inducement with the words
'Get on'. Then he slows down again, maintaining the same
direction. Arm movements are avoided, to render the distinction
from reconnaissance more evident. When the dog finds that it
is entirely released, i.e. no longer on any particular training-
ground, still less in a training-room, he will usually, in his
delight at the permission granted him to leave his confinement
at the trainer's side, make use of his new freedom at a leaping
gallop. If he does not do so—timid or frightened dogs keep
close to the trainer—the behaviour desired cannot be imposed
by compulsion. Its employment would render the animal still
more intimidated: he would hide behind the trainer or even
run away. For this reason inducement can only be practised in
the form of encouragement. If the secondary inducement, 'Get
on', proves effective when used alone, the primary inducement
is only resorted to in case of need.

Attention should be drawn to certain undesirable associations which may easily arise during training.

The dog should not be allowed to run ahead immediately after release from the lead, i.e. should not at once renounce obedience to it, otherwise an association may be formed between the visual stimulus of the detached lead and the reaction of running ahead. Detachment of the lead will then come to have the same meaning for the animal as 'Get on', causing it immediately to dash away on receipt of the visual stimulus, contrary to the trainer's intention. If, therefore, one wishes to allow a dog on the lead to run ahead, a time interval must ensue between detachment of the lead and the sound 'Get on'. The dog should also often be released without being allowed to run ahead.

If the dog has run on ahead, he should neither at once be called back nor immediately be made to stop what he is doing. For the association of exercises involving compulsion, with running ahead would change the meaning of the latter, causing it to be regarded as no longer true freedom. It would then be impossible to secure spontaneous running ahead. A time interval must therefore be introduced between running ahead and recall, or between running ahead and ceasing action.

(c) *Sitting*.
Auditory signal: 'Sit'.

Service requirement: At the word 'Sit' the dog has to sit down without hesitation.

One hand grasps the dog under the chest, the other is laid on the hindquarters. By means of appropriate pressure by both hands the dog is made to assume the seated posture, to the sound of the word 'Sit'. As soon as the dog has become accustomed to being made to sit down in this way, one hand, instead of grasping him under the chest, takes hold of the collar, near the nape, or else the lead is given a pull, so as to lift the dog slightly, while the other hand presses down the hindquarters and gets the animal down in that way—to the sound of the word 'Sit' as before. At a later stage 'Sit' or a slight jerk of the lead will suffice as secondary inducement.

The trainer remains in the immediate neighbourhood, so as to be able, by the use of the word 'Sit', instantly to prevent the dog getting up when he shows the least disposition to do so.

At this point we may ask whether the dog which has been made to adopt the seated posture through the compulsion exercised by this mechanical inducement should be encouraged, immediately after its conclusion, by 'There's a good boy' or fondling. The following advice was given in Chapter II. If the exercise begins with action and ends with abstention, no encouragement is administered in cases where the abstention required is in strong contrast to the dog's natural behaviour. Sitting is not one of these cases. It does, of course, consist of an action, sitting down, and a cessation from action, not getting up. But if sitting down and remaining seated are only required in the presence of the trainer, the dog does not experience the impulse to approach his pack-fellow, the man, which is deliberately created in him during the 'Down' exercise, when the man goes away from the dog. Consequently it is a matter of indifference, from the standpoint of ultimate effect, whether the compulsion imposed by the downward pressure is relieved by encouragement, or whether the compulsive effect is allowed to remain, the sound of encouragement or the fondling not being employed, after the dog has been made to sit.

In the case of the novice dog the following differences are occasionally found. At first the dog is made rather nervous by the downward pressure to which he is subjected, since he does not know what our intentions are. He does not recover from this uneasiness until the exercise has been repeated several times. He then finds that nothing disagreeable happens when he sits down and remains in that posture. And he becomes accustomed, eventually, to the downward pressure.

His interest in remaining seated is increased from the very outset owing to the fact that the nervousness induced by the downward pressure is not relieved by any form of encouragement. If, however, it occurs to the trainer that in the case, perhaps, of a timid animal, he would like to relieve this nervousness, which is only felt at the start of training and then only slightly, he may safely utter the phrase 'There's a good boy' to the dog immediately after he has exercised compulsion to make it sit. The encouragement received may cause the dog to rise, and this effect must be anticipated and instantly countered. It is important for the animal to learn that the encouragement given does not mean that he should get up.

Another primary inducement to sit may be applied, at an advanced stage of training, in the following way. Facing the dog, one takes him by the skin of the throat and gives his whole body a downward thrust, uttering the word 'Sit'. Practice in rapid sitting is finally undertaken and achieved by a swift downward pressure while uttering the word 'Sit'. As soon as the dog has learnt to adopt an attitude which will be to his advantage when he hears the call 'Sit', rapid sitting may also be induced by a light flick with the switch over the hindquarters.

For so long as the dog does not instantly sit down on the word being given, a matter which must receive close attention, repetition of the exercise should always include a primary inducement, made very rapidly, to oblige the animal to adopt this posture, accompanied simultaneously by the auditory signal as before. It frequently happens that the dog lies down of its own accord on receipt of the signal. This action should always be countered either by pulling the animal up with the lead or, preferably, by tapping very lightly the prostrate dog's toes, and at the same time pulling up the lead, which should always be employed with this inducement, and giving the command 'Sit'.

CHAPTER IV

DOWN AND RECALL EXERCISES

(a) GENERAL

IN THE down and recall the capacity of the dog to learn is reinforced by his submissive and pack instincts. The submissive instinct is of assistance in performing the actions of lying down and staying in that posture, while the pack instinct helps in the recall. On the trainer abandoning the animal after it has lain down, the latter, thus left alone, begins to feel the impulse to rejoin its human pack-fellow. This impulse can advantageously be used to contrive a rapid and willing recall by relieving the dog, with a call, of its loneliness. In this process the following consideration is to be borne in mind. The long down consists of lying down and remaining in that posture. A distinction should be made between lying down and remaining in that posture with strong distractions and remaining in the position in isolation. For example, the presumed culprit cornered by the dog may make an attempt to get away, or a hare may start up in front of the dog, the trainer in both cases being nearby. If the dog is then compelled by a call to lie down, the animal is not being left alone, for the trainer is close by. It would only begin to feel deserted if the trainer were distant at the time.

If the object of the training is to compel the dog, by calling from a distance, to lie down despite the presence of strong distractions, the lesson can only be learnt by the animal as the result of strict compulsion, as described in the following pages. It will be of additional assistance in this connection if no further exciting events as, for instance, a struggle with the presumed culprit, are allowed to occur after the down.

An isolated dog is assisted in maintaining his prostrate posture if he finds that after remaining down he is not called away but is fetched from the place where he is lying by the trainer. By this procedure the powerful recall impulse is prevented from arising, as is the tension which endangers the prostrate posture if the dog is regularly called away after being left. The procedure may vary according to the object of the training. If no special importance is attached to a reliable maintenance of the prostrate posture, or if the down is being employed as a means of obtaining rapid and willing recall, the animal may be called from the place in which he is lying. If the dog is already accustomed to this procedure and it is desired, as a primary object, to obtain reliable maintenance of the prostrate posture, calling away after the down is dispensed with, and the prostrate animal is regularly fetched from the place where he has been left.

In serious work, of course, procedure must depend on circumstances. If the correct inducements are used for the down and recall, the trainer obtains complete mastery over the dog. In the presence of powerful distractions it is easier to compel the animal, by uttering the word 'Down', to drop to the ground, than to bring him to one's side by uttering the word 'Here'. This is due to the ease with which strict compulsion can be exercised in teaching the down; such compulsion being less effective, as we shall see, in recall training.

(b) TEACHING THE DOWN

Auditory signal: 'Down'.

Service requirement: The dog, wherever he may be at the moment, whether standing, walking or running, has to throw himself to the ground, with lightning speed, at the word 'Down'. He has to remain prostrate, with his head up and mobile, until called away.

Since compulsion has to be employed without delay in this exercise, its effect is at first intimidating. But this effect is eliminated as soon as the dog has learnt that nothing disagreeable happens to him after he has lain down and while he remains in that posture. Until he has become accustomed to drop of his own accord on receipt of the secondary inducement, training should only take place on the lead. Otherwise the instinct of flight comes into play. The dog tries to escape the compulsion by flight, a reaction which must, under all circumstances, be prevented from the outset.

The use of the encouraging and intimidating sounds requires special consideration. The moment the dog begins to go down the trainer will probably feel impelled to praise him.

in other words to employ the sound of encouragement. But to do so may cause the dog to rise from the uncongenial posture he has assumed. If it is felt that the prostrate dog should be encouraged, possibly on account of excessive timidity, care must be taken to be in a position to force the animal down again instantly, if and when it rises. The following inducements should, then, be offered. The dog takes up the lying position. The trainer says, 'There's a good boy'. The animal shows a wish to rise. It is at once again forced to the ground by the word 'Down' (not 'Bah!'), succeeded by a further sound of encouragement, accompanied by a touch of the hand. It is of particular importance for the dog to learn not to rise at the word of encouragement. It is more advantageous, after training has reached an advanced stage, not to put an end to compulsion during the down. In this case the intimidation entailed, and not withdrawn, assists the maintenance of the prostrate posture.

Whenever the dog makes any attempt to rise prematurely, the usual sound of intimidation is not uttered, but only the word 'Down', which also has an intimidating effect, and thus, when accompanied by the primary inducement of downward pressure, compels the animal to lie down.

First Inducements.

One begins with a mild form of compulsion. The dog is gently pressed to the ground and held in that position. The manner in which he then lies at this stage does not matter. As soon as pressure commences the secondary inducement 'Down' is uttered in an admonitory tone. If it is also desired that the dog should obey a visual signal, the latter, for example a swift raising of the arm, accompanies the auditory signal from the start. The action being incomprehensible to the animal, he will at first wish to get up again, but is kept in position by continued repetition of the word 'Down'.

To enable the dog to learn the behaviour required, it is given the opportunity to repeat the behaviour which is not required. For this purpose the trainer's hands are raised a little. The moment the animal shows any sign of rising counter-tressure is renewed and the word 'Down' again pronounced. In phis way the dog finds standing up less congenial than lying

Alsatian stands still while handler searches 'criminal' for arms

Alsatian jumps to protect handler when he is attacked by 'criminal'

Man-work in full
protective clothing

Alsatian arrests 'criminal' who has attempted escape

down. The preliminary practice should only last a few minutes. If the undesirable behaviour is repeated, the trainer should resort to the primary inducement. He should not make the mistake of being tempted to substitute emphatic shouting for the downward pressure.

To avoid undue frightening, timid dogs may be allowed to rise of their own accord when the preliminary inducements are applied; the view taken here being that they should at first be familiarized only with the downward pressure.

Standing Up and Recalling.

As a primary inducement to stand up a jerk at the lead would suffice, but the recall which always immediately follows requires retreat by the trainer who, while jerking at the lead, quickly runs a few steps, then stoops with his face turned back towards the dog. Jerking at the lead and the backward movement are accompanied by the sound 'Here', always spoken in a high-pitched and caressing tone. When the dog reaches the trainer it should invariably be received with fondling and the phrase 'There's a good boy' (*see* Chapter V).

In down and recall training a constant switching is required from the disagreeable experience of lying down to the agreeable one of running to the handler. The more evident this alternation is made the more rapid and precise the progress of the animal will be.

Inducement to stand up is never applied until the dog is holding the prostrate posture *of its own accord*, without being touched by the trainer. At first it need maintain this position for only a few moments. On the other hand, every time the dog stands up of its own accord this movement must at once be countered again by downward pressure and the word 'Down'.

When the dog is reliable in lying down in the near neighbourhood of the trainer, attention should be paid to the following:

The primary inducement to stand up was provided by jerking the lead, and that to come by the trainer's rapid retreat. When these primary inducements to stand up and approach produce the results desired, it is possible and appropriate to resort to the secondary inducement 'Here' alone, in order to initiate standing up and approaching the handler. The dog then

E

concentrates only on the auditory signal 'Here'. As training proceeds, response to this type of inducement must be such that the dog pays no attention, on being put down, to any movement, however remarkable, on the part of the trainer, even if the latter runs or throws himself on the ground. The object is to render effective the word 'Here', as a signal to stand up and come to the trainer. But whenever the recall itself takes place hesitantly and with insufficient speed, the trainer may also resort to swift walking or running back in a stooping attitude as a primary inducement, always accompanying his actions with a caressingly pronounced 'Here'. It is necessary to get rid altogether of the idea that 'Here' is a command. It never becomes one. It is true that as training goes on it comes to have the same effect as a command, but we have not yet reached that stage.

The originally hesitant approach will, if the procedure here described is carefully followed, soon become an extremely rapid and willing one, especially as the distances to be covered grow longer. All other important aspects of the recall are dealt with in the following chapter.

Prevention of formation of an undesirable association.

Reference must now be made to an undesirable association which may easily arise. In the case of a novice dog, the down should never be undertaken while the dog is being called up or immediately after such action, otherwise, since the down involves strict compulsion, the dog will become shy in his recall, through expecting a threatening cry of 'Down!' In teaching the recall after the down the dog must, for this reason, always be treated with particular tenderness and an interval, with a change of location, should elapse before beginning a fresh inducement to down or any other act requiring compulsion.

Standing up of the dog's own accord must be rendered uncongenial.

In carrying out further exercises the following is of importance. One should always resort, so far as possible, to downward pressure and the word 'Down' at the very moment the dog shows signs of rising. It is the act of standing up that has to be rendered uncongenial to the animal. The trainer's eye must, therefore, always remain riveted to the dog.

Intensification of exercises.

Exercises are intensified by increased compulsion being applied to the tone of the word 'Down' and to the downward pressure. The animal is pressed downwards with a stronger and swifter movement.

The period of remaining prostrate is then gradually prolonged and the trainer begins to walk round the dog in wider and wider circles, even stepping over him, and finally retreating beyond the range of his scent and vision.

In intensifying exercises in this way the inexperienced trainer is recommended to make use of a long lead. To begin with this will enable him to keep the animal always under control. The end of the lead can be tied to a support, thus enabling the trainer to apply inducement from a distance by a jerk at the lead and the word 'Down', or to let the lead run through his hand while he dashes to the prematurely risen dog and presses him down again firmly.

The dog stands up prematurely when off the lead.

At the start of training without the lead special attention has to be paid to the tendency of the dog to stand up prematurely. If the animal is near, one makes a dash for him and presses him down again, uttering the word 'Down'. If this procedure is impossible, one merely calls out sharply, 'Down', without approaching the dog, for if one did so he would be inclined, instead of obeying the call, to evade it by taking to flight. If he does run away, the trainer must instantly change his tactics. He should walk rapidly or, preferably, run backwards and call out 'Here' in a caressing tone, encouraging the dog to come with frequent repetitions of 'There's a good boy' and receiving him in the usual friendly manner; stroking and fondling him as if nothing had happened.

To the anthropomorphic mind such behaviour may seem unreasonable. But one has to 'reason' as a dog does. If one were to punish the dog or show hostility to him for not retaining the prostrate position thereby causing him, as he approaches or after he has arrived, a disagreeable experience, he would not associate the punishment with the act of standing up, but with that of the recall and the word 'Here'. After a number of repetitions this association would become embedded in his memory and he would turn hand-shy.

Therefore, should the trainer be unable to intervene at once when premature rising takes place, he must effect a recall in the friendly manner described.

Similarly, one should not, as already mentioned, attempt to force the dog, with a perhaps even stricter form of compulsion, to perform the down immediately after the recall, since any association of the latter exercise with a subsequent disagreeable experience must be avoided. We must wait for a while, and fondle the dog, before bringing into operation the inducements described below.

The trainer runs with the dog, now attached to the long lead, which is, however, held within a few feet of the collar, and encouraging the animal by 'There's a good boy', to the place where the latter has been lying and there presses it to the ground, uttering the word 'Down' in a commanding manner. He may also, but not until a rather late stage of training, administer, not as a punishment but as a stricter form of compulsion, a flick with the switch on the dog's back *before he lies down*, as soon as the spot where he has been lying is reached. This action must be performed suddenly, with a flick of the wrist. The moment the switch touches the animal's back the word 'Down' must be uttered. *It is of great importance for these measures to coincide.* If the blow comes only a second later than the sound, the dog would try to avoid the blow on a future occasion. The sound 'Down' must come to have the meaning of a blow. It would not be advisable for an inexperienced trainer to apply this method of causing the dog to lie down unless the latter is on the lead. We need not worry about the cut with the switch causing the dog to develop shyness of the hand. This will occur only if the cut is given immediately after the recall. The sound 'Down' is intended to intimidate the dog.

The dog learns to stay down at any distance from the trainer.

Hitherto inducement to lie down has only been applied while the dog is near the trainer. When the habit has been so ingrained that the dog throws itself to the ground at the mere word 'Down', without any attempt at flight, we may proceed to dropping the dog when he is standing, walking or running at a distance from the trainer.

In this exercise the secondary inducement 'Down' alone is

employed, as before, occasionally accompanied by a gesture from the trainer.

The difficulties presented to the animal by distance and the presence of distractions are only very gradually increased. If the dog, instead of dropping on the word 'Down', runs away, it is not yet ready for these exercises. In these circumstances the trainer must at once change his tactics and call the dog in.

If, at the word 'Down' the dog is at a considerable distance from the trainer and in the face of very strong distractions, it is necessary, as stated earlier on and for reasons to be given presently, to resort to a strict form of compulsion, involving the instigation of alarm.

This measure may be effected without any interference with the animal's enjoyment of its work and without entailing the slightest risk of the dog becoming hand-shy. The strict form of compulsion should at first only be applied with the dog on the *short* lead. The object is to ensure that the only way the animal can avoid the disagreeable experience of a flick with the switch is by quickly throwing itself on the ground. This instantaneous movement should not have the character of an exhibition. It is rendered necessary in order that powerful distractions may be neutralized by still more powerful inducements.

The unsuspecting dog is held at the trainer's side by a lead which is kept quite short. He is unexpectedly struck by a sudden, very swift cut with the switch, effected by a flick of the wrist. This cut must be administered dexterously enough to prevent the dog noticing any preliminary movement of the trainer's body. The moment the switch touches the animal's back, neither earlier nor later, the word 'Down' must be given. A single cut only is required. It must be applied in a grazing fashion, so that the dog, as it drops, perceives that the weight of the blow has already diminished; that he can escape it entirely by instantaneous prostration and that he is immune as soon as he lies down. One cut only, therefore! When the dog lies down the trainer walks round him, without giving him any encouragement, to make sure that he retains the posture. If he does so, he may be released from the lead. The trainer then walks a dozen paces away and starts running backwards while calling 'Here' in a caressing tone. In this exercise it is advisable to use the long lead to begin with. The force of the cut depends on the character of the individual dog. The important point is dropping quickly. It is not expedient to repeat this exercise immediately. It should be practised at intervals in different places and invariably as a surprise, in order to avoid the formation of undesirable associations.

Even with the trained animal there must be resort, at intervals, to simultaneous employment of the cut and the word 'Down', otherwise the faculty of rapid prostration, and with it complete mastery of the dog, will be lost.

The dog should never be struck when it is already lying down. If it has not lain down quickly enough on any occasion when the word 'Down' is used alone, a cut may be applied, at the next training, on the down, but not before. Once the dog is lying down it must feel itself secure from any disagreeable experience at the hands of the trainer.

(c) Dropping on Command and Staying Down

When a dog has learnt to stay down, care must be taken never to allow him to get up before he is called, or fetched. Many owners are in the habit of using the word 'Down' when they are not concerned with making the dog really lie down. Even when he is down, the performance must be strictly supervised. If he is frequently allowed to stand up before being called or fetched, his unconditional retention of the prostrate posture will obviously be prejudiced. Indoors, when we only wish to keep the dog out of our way if he is being a nuisance, the word 'Down' should not, therefore, be used, for it would imply that for some reason or other we wish to make him stay down. But if all we desire is that the dog should go to the place where he usually lies, or lie down elsewhere in the room, a different inducement must be employed. We may, for example, say, with a threatening movement, 'Lie down'. The animal will then go to his usual place and there is no need for anything more.

CHAPTER V

SPECIAL INSTRUCTIONS ON THE RECALL

AUDITORY signal: 'Here' or a whistle.

There is no service required from the dog in which mistaken interpretations of canine behaviour cause such distressing consequences as in the recall. The errors so frequently committed in the inducements applied in teaching the recall lead to the very opposite of what is desired. Instead of the dog dashing up to his master in a swift, joyful rush, it approaches him timidly, slowly and hesitantly.

A dog may be seen standing at some distance from its angrily shouting owner with shrinking hindquarters and its tail between its legs. It does not dare to come within his reach and repeatedly eludes the hand that tries to grasp it. The owner, by this time exasperated or, if temperamental, in a blind fury, may now approach the dog, scolding it; whereupon the animal will take to its heels. In this way dogs are made hand-shy. The final act of the tragedy is played when the dog has run home and is there given belated punishment for his 'disobedience'. His clearly recognizable 'guilty conscience'—such is the expression used—is regarded as deserving such treatment.

Though the dog succeeded in eluding the menace of his angrily shouting owner by flight, he nevertheless has to endure belated punishment inflicted upon him at home, as does a slave tormented without reason, out of sheer caprice. The long lapse of time between the 'disobedience' of his failure to come and the punishment forbids (the gap being unbridgeable by canine understanding) the formation of any association with behaviour in the past. In other words, the dog has been given no chance to learn its lesson, quite apart from the fact that punishment for failure to come when called is always inopportune. Yet it is by no means uncommon for dog training to be carried out in this mistaken fashion, as though the pupil were a child which could be dealt with by the use of language. For a child at this stage the word 'Come' suggests an order. If it is not obeyed, we may say: 'If you don't come, you'll be punished' or, hours afterwards explain, 'As you didn't come, you're now going to be punished.' This kind of treatment, covering either the future or the past, is wholly inapplicable with dogs. Dogs cannot speak or understand language. They are unable to form ideas and, therefore, have no conception of orders, obedience, duty, guilt, blame and punishment, praise and reward. They have nothing to do with any kind of morality, or with good and evil.

The fact that training enables us to make a dog obey, as if in response to an order, is due to a different cause. The degree in which the demands we make upon a dog are successful depends on how closely they approach his innate modes of behaviour, which arise from his instincts.

Ever since the dog lived in a state of nature, as a wild animal of wolf type in packs, the pack instinct, or sociable impulse, has dwelt within him, exercising an inner compulsion upon him to remain in close association with his fellows. His life with human beings, when he belongs to a family circle, resembles life in a pack. A dog's dependence on man is the expression of his pack instinct. He suffers greatly if he is left alone for any length of time. It is owing to this pack instinct that we are able to train the dog, unlike the solitary cat, to come when he is called with so little trouble.

We require from him something quite outside his instinctive range, viz. unconditional obedience to the recall in any circumstances, however strong may be the distractions that tempt him to leave his master's side. This requirement does not correspond with any natural conduct in the dog, so it must be learnt, and learnt through compulsion, which is always necessary in cases where the dog does not spontaneously carry out what is required of him.

In this dilemma we are assisted by a further instinct, in addition to that of the pack, which has descended from the dog's past and is innate in him. This is his readiness to adopt a certain rank within the pack. In a pack of wild dogs the leader has despotic power and all the members of the pack are subordinate to him. The human being takes the place of the pack-leader. The dog is content to be unconditionally subordinate to him, provided inducements to be so are imposed *in the manner in which they are imposed by the pack-leader*. But this general subordination does not ensure that a special performance like that of the recall will at once be satisfactorily executed. It has to be learnt.

A man, in his capacity of pack-leader, and a dog, as a member of his pack—not on the lead when training begins—may be walking in a field. Both suddenly catch sight of a running hare. Even if the dog has already been taught the recall he will dash after the hare, however much his trainer may call and whistle.

The dog has no idea of the duty to return to his master. The instinct of the chase has been aroused. It has far greater attractive power than the call or the whistle. Nature commands, 'Go for that hare!' If the dog could think he would consider that his human pack-leader had hopelessly degenerated, since he did not join in the chase.

After pursuit of the hare has proved unsuccessful the hunting instinct ceases to operate and the pack instinct is aroused. The dog, therefore, starts to move towards his master. He would normally trot up quite placidly and jump up on the man in his pleasure at being united with him once more. But something unpleasant and unexpected happens. Before he gets near the man, shouts ring out and the events which have already been described are repeated. The 'guilty conscience' of the dog is again made an excuse for punishment.

Wilhelm Busch, in his German children's classic *Max and Moritz*, has brilliantly illustrated this subject, without of course having in mind the topic we are now dealing with. Max and Moritz steal, from the roof of the house, the chickens which the widow Bolte has put on to cook, by fishing them up one after the other through the chimney. The gallant little Pomeranian does all he can to foil the rascals by barking for all he is worth (*see* Fig. 3). When, however, the widow returns to her kitchen she thinks the dog is the thief and behaves accordingly. At her scolding words and threatening gestures the Pom immediately assumes a 'guilty' look (*see* Fig. 4) which increases when the widow Bolte rushes to attack the poor animal, which is absolutely innocent (*see* Fig. 5). The infliction of punishment some considerable time after the supposed misdeed, concludes this monstrous scene (*see* Fig. 6).

The 'guilty conscience' is caused simply and solely by the

so called fear inspired by the menacing noises and gestures of
the human being. In fact the dog's 'conscience' is quite 'clear'.
Such fear is always aroused in the dog by hostile behaviour on
the part of its master. For, as a rule, the animal has had it
knocked into his memory from puppyhood that hostile human

FIG. 3

attitudes are accompanied, or quickly followed, by some disagreeable experience. But the cause of fear in the presence of
the master is never awareness in the dog of any present, let
alone any past, behaviour to which the man objected.

The case of the widow Bolte does not, of course, cover all
cases of fear of a master being aroused. Threats of this very
obvious kind, presaging trouble, are not at all necessary to
provoke it. One has only to be vexed with the dog, without
saying a word, and fear may well ensue. This is not because the

FIG. 4

FIG. 5

FIG. 6

dog is a thought-reader. He is, however, a first-rate observer, far superior to ourselves, of movement and consequently capable of noticing even the slightest of our physical movements and attitudes. Our hostile or friendly state of mind is perfectly evident to the dog, for human emotions are usually, though often unconsciously, accompanied by physical actions and postures.

If one wishes to provoke an appearance of 'guilt', i.e. fear, in the dog deliberately, one has to take care to give one's physical movements and attitudes the same character as they would have in genuine exasperation. On the other hand, a dog will become aware of human exasperation when one is putting on an act, with an outward expression of good humour but experiencing an inward one of annoyance. The human being is by no means a perfect dissembler along these lines.

But fear can also arise after a misdeed even when we are genuinely well disposed to the dog and let him see it. This may happen in the following way: let us assume that a dog has repeatedly had disagreeable experiences in the past, after approaching his master. For example, he may have chased a cat or eaten something that was not meant for him and the disagreeable experience may have occurred not at the time such undesirable behaviour took place but only after its conclusion and out of sight or scent of the objects which provoked it. In such circumstances the dog's bad conduct would not be made to seem unpleasant to him. Chasing the cat, or whatever it may have been, would retain its pleasurable aspect; the unpleasantness would be attributed to what followed.

A 'bad conscience'—for this expression read 'fear'—in the presence of the master arises, in the first place, as a consequence of the hostility expressed in the latter's voice, bodily attitude and movements, in the form of foreboding. A genuinely friendly bearing of the man will also cause it in the form of retrospective terror, if the dog has repeatedly had an unpleasant experience after he has behaved in a certain way.

Both these forms of fear have a particularly unfortunate influence on the recall. They may, however, be completely avoided by the employment of the correct inducements.

Any signs of the dog not progressing with the recall should at once be regarded as evidence of wrongly directed inducement. Let us suppose that the rules laid down in the foregoing pages are being observed, but that they have not been applied in earlier training. Some considerable time will then be required to remove the animal's inhibitions. For fear complexes once formed can only be eliminated, particularly in the case of older dogs, by the exercise of almost angelic patience. Behaviour in the manner of the widow Bolte will ruin a good recall more effectively than anything. Attention must be drawn, too, to another point. If a dog at one time seems pleased and at another worried during the recall, it means that our poor friend is in a hopeless state of confusion. Advantage and disadvantage have become entangled, causing that all too familiar hesitant attitude of the dog which may so easily lead us to mistaken conclusions. The animal feels half attracted and half repelled. He cannot unravel the chaotic state of his emotions and is thus unable to discern where his advantage lies. It is an all important first principle, therefore, that, whether the dog comes to his master after behaving in a desirable or in an undesirable way, it must always be given an agreeable experience and a friendly reception at the moment of arrival. We must ensure that the recall is made a thoroughly enjoyable act. In order to lend to the sound 'Here' and the whistle, a power of attraction which will meet all requirements, we must employ methods suited to canine understanding.

To begin with, it will be as well to understand clearly, once and for all, that the dog has no sense of duty. Such anthropomorphic notions continually cause us to apply the wrong kind of inducement, for, however warm may be the feelings of a human being towards a dog, they run the risk of becoming drastically chilled if the animal is assumed to have any kind of insight into the reason for our inducements or any idea of morality. Goodwill is thenceforward replaced by malice and this wrongly conceived attitude involves the taking of compulsive measures which cause a great deal of suffering to an innocent animal and defeat our purpose into the bargain.

In dealing with a dog we have nothing to consider but *the giving to him of pleasure or displeasure by our acts and the proper apportionment of agreeable and disagreeable experiences.*

Disagreeable experiences, the reasons for which could only be impressed on a creature capable of understanding human speech, include tying up, locking in, the withholding of food, refusal to speak to the dog and so on. These penalties have only a depressive effect, and they cannot help in training. If such experiences are frequently repeated, the dog loses confidence in its master and often expresses this loss by showing fear in his presence.

Disagreeable experiences which we impose upon the dog for educational purposes are known as compulsion. It is used in the most diverse degrees, from weak to strong, from a slightly menacing tone in the pronouncement of auditory signals to the infliction of pain, corresponding with the character of the individual dog and the sort of service required. These experiences have an intimidating effect and consequently cause cessation of the behaviour for which they are imposed. Agreeable experiences, on the other hand, encourage the animal and consequently cause continuation of the behaviour concerned.

Agreeable experiences include the—always abrupt—arrest of compulsion the moment the dog shows the least sign of performing the service required.

The sudden cessation of compulsion may not always bring about the performance of the desired action when this involves a form of behaviour which has to be induced and rendered congenial. The cessation of compulsion must then be made to coincide with introduction of an agreeable experience. This consists in the employment of the sound of encouragement, to which we shall refer again in a moment, and the caressingly accented auditory signal sometimes used, as well as in fondling the dog, or in the offering of morsels of food.

The sharp contrast between the disagreeable experience (compulsion) and the agreeable, bringing abruptly changing emotions of distress and pleasure, administered in accordance with the canine behaviour at the time, makes it easy for the animal to appreciate where his advantage lies, and he learns very quickly.

In addition to this kind of adjustment to canine understanding an equally important preliminary condition for rapid learning is that the dog is kept in a good temper by the study of his emotional and instinctive life.

The ideal is to ensure that the dog never experiences depression for any length of time. Depression is the enemy of all action, while good humour is a powerful incentive to activity.

Unfortunately it is not ordinarily feasible at the commencement of a course of methodical training to prevent depression from ever occurring, especially in sensitive dogs. Even in the case of working dogs a strict form of compulsion cannot always be dispensed with. All we can do, therefore, is to restrict depression as much as possible.

We shall do so by making the change between the disagreeable and the agreeable experience rapid and abrupt. An exercise may become for the dog, associated as it is with compulsion, conspicuously uncongenial; but by the means suggested the association of discomfort is restricted to the exercise itself and not transferred to the trainer. There is also the additional factor that the amiability of the trainer, which causes the dog to trust him, must be permanent, transcending everything else and never more than briefly interrupted by compulsion.

A further requisite in making the dog take pleasure in its work, is to see that, so far as possible, its instinctive behaviour is called on in coping with the lesson, thus permitting the inward impulse of the dog to come into play.

Finally, every opportunity should be taken to relieve a depressed state without delay. For this purpose the part, necessary in itself, of a human pack-leader employing compulsion, must be replaced by that of a playful pack-companion of equal rank.

This interchange of parts is an important matter to the dog. Those who understand canine mentality make the change-over from pack-leader to companion extremely rapid, so that the instinct of play comes into operation at once. Necessary features of the performance are very short, jerky movements of the body forwards and backwards, to and fro, as if making, by turns, playful attacks or attempts at flight. One has to behave precisely as dogs themselves do at play.

This kind of amusement is also promoted by the utterance of the caressingly accented play-call, at the top of one's voice. The repetition of a noise of this kind, e.g. a long-drawn 'hey-hey-hey-hey-hey-hey-hey-hey', has a most stimulating effect.

The uninitiated may consider this adoption of playful hilarity with the animal ridiculous. But our aim is to establish a good understanding between man and dog, and this can only be achieved by putting ourselves on the same level with the animal. 'Dad' and 'Mum' often behave rather strangely when playing with their infant; their sole purpose being to give it pleasure, irrespective of how their behaviour may appear to others.

We may also bring about the continuance or cessation of an action by using the two expressions 'Bah!' and 'There's a good boy' by way of intimidation or encouragement, but never to convey blame or praise.

The sudden alternation between agreeable and disagreeable experiences which has been recommended is particularly difficult for those who are fond of dogs, yet find it impossible to get rid of their anthropomorphic prepossessions. Such people have their hands tied by the ideas of praise and reward, blame and punishment. These human means to education cannot of course be used with such abrupt transitions as the provision of agreeable and disagreeable experiences. One cannot imagine oneself praising and blaming, or punishing and rewarding, in the same breath, a child that understands human speech.

There are, however, occasions in human life when we do employ abrupt alternation in cases of desirable or undesirable behaviour. Children who are playing 'hunt the thimble' or some such game are often guided in their search by someone who knows where the thimble is hidden. If the child gets near the hiding-place, a certain expression, such as 'hot', is used, which may be regarded as the equivalent to 'There's a good boy', and another, 'cold', which may be likened to 'Bah!', is employed, if the child moves away from the hiding-place. Such expressions are often used in rapid succession, as the child moves close to or away from the hidden object. We behave in exactly the same way with the alternation of agreeable or disagreeable experiences in the case of a dog, according to whether his behaviour corresponds or is at variance with the object of training.

It has already been explained that a dog approaching his trainer must be shown that a warm welcome awaits him, for it is only in the expectation of such a welcome that he will come with any speed. To appreciate this exercise better we will divide it into two parts. The first begins with the inducement to come and extends to the point at which the animal comes into contact with his trainer as he runs towards him. The second comprises the inducements offered after the dog's arrival.

We may get a better idea of the way in which the recall comes to be performed, if we compare this process with that of teaching heel on lead. Each time the dog on the lead moves away from the left side of the trainer he is jerked back again by the lead. This is the primary inducement given. The jerk on the lead is a form of compulsion, experienced by the animal as disagreeable and intimidating, which after several repetitions causes straying from the trainer's left side to be abandoned. Each time the dog is jerked back the compulsion definitely ceases and the sound of encouragement, which is accompanied by fondling, provides an actively agreeable experience. The dog thus finds it to his advantage to remain at the trainer's left side. This locality comes to be regarded by the animal as a refuge from discomfort; a place where he finds security as soon as he hears the sound 'Heel'.

The point is that the dog must learn to do what is required in response to an auditory or visual signal. For this purpose, right from the start, a certain sound must be made at the same time as the primary inducement is given by the lead. (Visual signals are usually dispensed with in heel work.) The sound 'Heel' is at first quite ineffective. It is only after several repetitions that this noise begins to be associated with the movement that jerks the animal to the man's left side and with staying in that position. The word 'Heel' then becomes a secondary inducement. The association thus formed through memory causes the sound 'Heel', used by itself, to evoke the same response as was originally effected only by the primary inducement.

Substantial differences, however, exist in the psychological composition of the separate exercises required from the dog. From this point of view heel on lead contrasts with the recall.

In teaching the former the led dog remains permanently under the trainer's control, so that each of the primary inducements required for learning the lesson, which mainly consist in jerking the dog to the left side of the trainer, has the effect desired. A further advantage is that the employment of compulsion at the right moment, and to the right extent, works almost automatically. Jerk—pull—we achieve our object in the simplest possible way and the dog pulled to our left side is let alone so long as he stays where he is.

In these circumstances mistaken conceptions of the man and

F

dog relationship cannot have nearly such a harmful effect as could result in teaching the recall. It then often happens that the dog is off the lead and may be a long distance from his master, so that he is peculiarly at the mercy of distractions. Consequently, a considerable period of training must elapse, in contrast with teaching heel on lead, before the primary induce-ments (which have yet to be specified) can in every case succeed with the unattached animal, to say nothing of such secondary ones as the call 'Here' or a whistle, which are at first nothing but meaningless echoes in the dog's ears.

The fact is that we are not able to impose inducements on a dog that is off the lead in such a way that he will always behave in accordance with our wishes. The necessity for training with-out the lead is one of the special difficulties encountered in mastering the recall. It is true that we may use the long lead, but the latter is only an auxiliary resource, insufficient in itself to achieve the object of training.

Another particularly difficult feature in teaching the recall is the correct use of compulsion. For we shall not succeed, with-out appropriate compulsion, in securing thoroughly reliable performance.

Compulsion can never be employed in recall training until just before the dog meets its master, in other words it can only be used *in the first phase of the welcome. The dog must never, throughout its life, have any—even the slightest—disagreeable ex-perience on coming into physical contact with its master.* Nothing other than a friendly reception, consisting in fondling and the utterance of sounds of encouragement, must ever be given. Even the mildest form of compulsion, e.g. a commanding 'Here', such as is always accompanied by a menacing bodily attitude, frightens the animal and causes inhibitions in coming up until he is reassured. Any compulsion applied must be relieved immediately it has achieved its object.

The sound of encouragement and other inducements, which still remain to be specified, must be employed to eliminate the fear provoked and restore the animal's zest and confidence. To express this matter more clearly we may say that so long as a sword of Damocles, in the form of threatening sounds and movements, is hanging over the dog he is bound to feel anxiety, especially if he knows from experience that he is in for a bad time as soon as he gets to his trainer. Any creature on earth would be repelled by such a feeling.

So much then for the use of compulsion in teaching the recall. We may now recall the case in which a dog accompanying his master across a field dashes after a flying hare and, again deliberately to use an anthropomorphic expression, is quite astounded when his human pack-leader, instead of joining in the chase, incomprehensibly takes no notice of it and stays where he is.

The impulse innate in a hunting beast of prey like a dog to chase anything that moves rapidly away from him is employed

FIG. 7
Running backwards from dog

as one of the main attractive forces in teaching the recall. It is then the human pack-leader who takes over the part of the flying hare, though without, of course, exercising the same powerful attraction. The man runs, like the hare, away from the dog. With his face turned towards the animal, he moves backwards as fast as possible, in a straight line, while at the same time the dog's ear catches the successive sounds, uttered in extremely loud and caressing tones, of 'Here'. (*See* Fig. 7.), The trainer's backward run and also the accompanying calls of 'Here' last until the animal reaches the man and touches him when it is invariably greeted in friendly fashion.

If necessary, the attractive force of this backward run may be increased by the trainer making long leaps away from the dog, with his back turned to it this time, keeping the direction straight. Deviations, as well as looking round, and thus interrupting or slowing down the backward run, decrease the attraction of the latter, especially when the dog has been rendered uneasy by some disagreeable experience that took place shortly before. In such circumstances, the modifications referred to in the backward run will operate as if they were the renewal of a hostile attitude.

The backward run from the dog affects two instincts: the pack instinct and that of the chase. If, for instance, the pack-leader begins to run, the impulse arises in its pack companions to keep within the pack. Moreover, any movement of the pack-leader stimulates, the more powerfully the faster it is, both the psychological and physical elements in the other members of the pack, for the commencement of a rapid gait is associated with the chase or some other exciting event. If only everyone who is fond of dogs could be convinced of the power, and the effects it can produce, residing in human bodily attitudes and movements!

Let us now take a closer view of actual practical training.

Since it is the man who is conducting it, we must first deal with him. As we have already seen, a benevolent attitude to the dog, which must never be relaxed, is the indispensable and ruling principle of teaching the recall. We shall the more easily maintain it the more accurately we understand true canine nature. Once we lose our self-control—and we shall frequently be put to the test—the results of all our painstaking work may be lost and a cruel injustice be done to the dog.

Let us once more make certain that we understand the following axiom. The final object of training, in the case of the recall, is that the dog should come quickly and cheerfully to his master in response to a secondary inducement alone, either the call 'Here' or a whistle, and of course *invariably* come quite close up to him.

Prior to the formation of this habit, primary inducements compose the attractive forces required. One of the latter, the backward run from the dog, has already been mentioned.

It is important to pay attention to the following point. Successful instruction depends partly upon the simultaneous use of secondary and primary inducements. We may exemplify the point by reference to the primary inducement employed in the backward run. In the case of a novice dog any backward run by the trainer in the absence of a simultaneous 'Here' or whistle would be ineffective. Premature and isolated use of the word 'Here' or the whistle would also be wrong. Premature use may be recognized by the fact that the dog does not come so briskly as when the primary inducement is used at the same time. It shows that the association desired between the word 'Here' or the whistle and the reaction to come has not yet become sufficiently stable. There is no question of 'perversity' on the part of the dog.

Those who assume such 'perversity' become excited and try, by shouting at the dog and executing movements expressive of menace, or by advancing upon the dog at a run or a walk, to compel the animal to approach more quickly. Quite apart from the fact that any advance upon the dog made in anger arouses the latter's instinct of flight, and thus in the end produces the very opposite effect from that desired, we forget, in our anger, to relieve the dog's anxiety and the menacing figure of Wilhelm Busch's widow Bolte, so to speak, stands over the wretched animal.

The primary inducements are only toned down very gradually.

In the case of the backward run the distance is abbreviated and the speed slackened, until at last the run is merely indicated by its initial physical movements. In calling, the loud tones are lowered by degrees to normal and the caressing accent progressively attenuated. The dog is always closely watched as it approaches, and the primary inducement is immediately resorted to again and its attractive power intensified as it becomes necessary.

Many dogs are strongly attracted—we may call this an extra primary inducement—if we reduce our bulk by crouching as low as possible, for example by actually kneeling or even lying full length on the ground. We may welcome the dog while remaining in this posture.

Two exercises which include the run back as a primary inducement are to be distinguished. The first is teaching the recall combined with the down, and the second is calling the dog while off the lead but quite near to his master.

In teaching the down the latter exercise may be suitably combined with the recall from the very first day. When the dog is left to itself, it feels lonely. The trainer, as he walks away, arouses the impulse in the animal to rejoin his master. This impulse grows as the distance and the period of absence lengthen. It is a happy release for the dog thus left to itself when it is able, in accordance with the pack instinct, to rejoin its master.

The psychological state of the dog, when left alone, affords an excellent opportunity for obtaining an enthusiastic and rapid recall and lays a first-rate foundation for forming the habit of doing so. If on such occasions the run back is also used, this auxiliary expedient considerably enhances the attractive power coming from the master.

When first teaching the down, with master and dog quite close to each other and the latter still on the lead, the primary inducement, implying permission to stand up and come, is actually given by a jerk at the lead, accompanied by a simultaneous, caressingly uttered 'Here'. If the run back is also added, at the same time, to these two inducements, it operates as the decisive attractive force, encouraging the dog to come quickly. It is true that by this procedure we have to accept an undesirable association, that of the run back as a sign to come, accompanying as it does the other inducements. This slight drawback may however be accepted without misgiving. The association is dispersed as the distances increase and the run is omitted, or only resorted to during the recall itself if the latter leaves something to be desired.

The ultimate aim of the down is of course that the dog should only come at a call or whistle and remain prostrate, while the master runs away.

Running backwards is indispensable for recall instruction in the case of a dog off the lead, moving about close to his master and feeling at liberty. Such exercises may be used with even quite young dogs when they are first taken out. In this case the psychological state of the dog differs from that pertaining to the down and must be borne in mind.

When the dog is not left to itself and, therefore, is not lonely, but is running free, the animal's senses and desires are not exclusively directed upon his master, as they are when down. A dog off the lead is preoccupied with its own affairs.

What we call distractions, for instance a cat running away, may possess a considerably stronger attractive force for a dog being taught the recall than all the inducements his master can offer. Hence arises the need to strengthen the inducements provided by the man to such an extent that they outweigh all distractions, but we can only gradually meet this requirement. In the days of training by force, which one shudders to think of, the following were the guiding principles in the drill imposed. First the dog must grasp the idea of obedience. All resistance by the animal must be broken by the strictest form of compulsion, such as the use of the whip and the spiked collar. This requirement had to be met by means of drill in a room from which the dog could not escape.

As consciously contrived resistance by a dog only exists in the imagination of human beings, the excessive and unnecessary compulsion was exercised in a wholly mistaken fashion. As a result, the dog became utterly cowed the moment it entered the training-room and its timidity, as usual, rendered it extraordinarily difficult to teach. Its sufferings under this superfluous drill must have been appalling. Indeed, from a technical point of view, the recall can never be properly taught in a room, which affords no opportunity for the exercise of the pack instinct. And what becomes of a dog's natural enthusiasm in a training-room, where it has to learn all the other rigorous disciplines into which compulsion enters?

Yet this enthusiasm is just what we need.

Depression can even overwhelm a dog when he is taken to a training-ground in the open, where he is taught submission by means involving compulsion. His recollection of previous compulsion is responsible for this condition. Backward running practice with the dog off the lead cannot be undertaken in such places. The animal would either remain close to his master or rush away from him. The backward run is best practised when the dog is taken to localities where he has never experienced compulsion of any kind. Powerful distractions must, however, be absent from such a neighbourhood. If a distraction should occur which attracts the dog more than the run back, one should prevent its operation, if possible, by putting the dog on the lead before he notices it. If it is too late for this procedure and the backward run, combined with the word 'Here', does not result in approach, one is left, at this stage of training, quite without control over the dog. The sooner this is fully understood the better. In such circumstances, as for instance when the animal chases a hare, we can do nothing, but when the dog eventually rejoins his master of his own accord, he must be welcomed with the backward run and invariably received in friendly fashion.

When the backward run is being practised with a dog off the lead, it does not matter, at the start of instruction, whether the animal is in front, to the side of or behind his trainer. All that is necessary is for the dog to be some paces distant from the man and able to see the latter run back. The first few exercises should be begun while the dog is actually looking at his trainer, or else the animal's attention should be attracted by a clearly audible sound, such as is produced by a vigorous slap on one's knee. After a few repetitions the word 'Here', which will, of course, always be uttered in conjunction with the backward run, will cause the dog to look towards his trainer. On arrival, the dog reaches the second phase of enjoyment. As has several times been emphasized, the dog grasps neither the sense nor the object of what is required of him, but only its external succession of events in time and space. When, therefore, immediately on arrival, something disagreeable occurs, this experience will tend to give the recall an unpleasant character. In other words an undesirable association will be formed, leading to inhibited recall. Consequently, exercises involving compulsion should never be undertaken immediately after the recall. Further details on this point will be given when we describe the second phase of enjoyment.

It is also necessary for the dog to be released immediately after being given his due welcome and for the auditory signal which we employ when the dog is at liberty to be used. The primary inducement given by the trainer running a few paces forward is then of particular importance in dealing with a novice dog.

The dog's feeling of being at liberty would be obliterated, if the recall follows running ahead at too short an interval. The abatement of this feeling may be recognized if the dog no longer runs off happily when his master sets him at liberty after being recalled. A mild form of compulsion, consisting in the use of the intimidating exclamation 'Bah!' and a sharply uttered 'Here', may begin soon after the back-run exercises start. One should never forget to relieve compulsion by employing the sound of encouragement 'There's a good boy'. It will often be necessary to switch abruptly from 'Bah!' to 'There's a good boy' and back again. But this mild compulsion offers us no protection from the attractive power of strong distractions. Strict compulsion is indispensable for that purpose. At this point we reach the most delicate stage in teaching the recall.

At the stage when the dog is already happily running to its master, as a result of having invariably enjoyed pleasurable experiences on making its approach, the most effective means we can think of for the reinforcement of the sounds 'Here' and the whistle would be some measure which would enable us to give it a fright, however distant it might be. The moment the feeling of alarm begins and ceases a caressing 'Here' would be uttered and as soon as the frightened animal looked at its master the run back, accompanied by repetition of the word 'Here', would be initiated. With these inducements the dog, even if exposed to the most powerful distractions, would learn to put them aside and run to its master. Such a measure would be ideal for eliminating all the difficulties connected with the achievement of a reliable recall. What substitute can we make use of in place of this imaginary resource?

The first expedient is the use of the long lead.

Just as, in practice with the lead, the primary inducement given by pulling in the lead succeeds in every case, such an inducement given with the long lead might succeed when we are dealing with the recall. It is possible, by use of the word 'Here', the run back and the friendly reception, to attract a dog from some distance away. But the series of events consisting of putting the dog on the lead, retreating from him and pulling him in, or simply the dog's awareness of being on the long lead, would soon cause the animal to remain obstinately at his master's side. Moreover, the recall taught with the long lead alone would only succeed while the dog was on the lead. With the animal off the lead training would be impossible.

This limitation may be overcome to some extent if we use the long lead only in cases when the dog is highly excited by a distraction, for he then pays no attention to the fact that he is on the lead. This happens, for example, when the dog is learning to work on the 'criminal' and, while angrily barking, is called back. On such occasions a strong jerk at the lead is given to the sound of 'Here', and the dog is pulled in as the trainer runs backwards.

The long lead may also be used with dogs that have been spoilt by mistaken inducements. It may be of service, too, in breaking the dog of undesirable habits, for example reversion to a state of nature, hostility to cats and so on. For these purposes the dog is taken on the long lead, which is, however, held short, as in ordinary heel work, to places where the distractions in mind are to be found. On the dog taking notice of one he is set at liberty by allowing the lead to run out. As soon as the tightened lead causes a powerful jerk, which may be reinforced by a simultaneous backward jerk administered by the trainer, the dog sustains a shock and the recall inducements already described can be applied.

In this case, the shock felt by the dog is of assistance in lending urgency to the simultaneous sounds of 'Here' or the whistle. Consequently, when combined with the backward run, this shock substantially improves reliability in the recall and will often break the animal of undesirable habits.

Nevertheless, as already stated, comprehensive perfection in the recall is not obtainable by means of the long lead. From the dog's point of view recall when he is off the lead is quite a different matter, especially in the presence of strong distractions. Our control of the dog is limited so long as we lack the ideal measure already mentioned.

The limits of our control do not extend far beyond the distances within which we can alarm the animal. This is particularly the case with tough dogs having a strong pack-leader instinct and a weak pack instinct.

Our range for the administration of alarm at a distance will depend on the one hand on that of the means at our disposal and on the other on the trainer's adroitness in making use of such means.

An advocate of training by force recommends for the 'reformation of dogs which have deteriorated' the 'disciplinary shot', fired from a gun, and draws attention to the 'moral effect' of this expedient. If the dog, contrary to the man's wishes, pursues a fleeing hare, he is peppered with the pellets of the 'disciplinary shot'. Such barbarous procedure cannot be advocated. From the point of view of pure theory this method may be correct in its administration of alarm and pain at the moment of the action that the dog is to be made to discontinue. In practice, however, the method has an adverse effect, as the pain inflicted by the wounds may last a considerable time. Yet it will not be possible, in that case, to restrict the requisite disagreeable experience applied to the animal.

That one falls into further error with regard to the effect of this method is evident from these basic assumptions: "Immediately after the disciplinary shot the dog should be whistled in, put on the lead and vigorously chastised with the spiked collar and the whip, to make him realize that the shot was meant for him." This is, of course, to give an outrageously human character to canine understanding and implies an utter misconception of the possible relationship between man and dog.

The further punishment recommended, after the 'disciplinary shot' and the arrival of the dog, while the latter is entirely guiltless, can naturally only be associated by the animal with the recall, for the dog has not the remotest idea why pain is inflicted upon him. A realization by the dog that it was his master that gave him the pain cannot be brought about in this manner, and it is of course totally undesirable that it should be.

If one is in a position, in certain cases during training, to give the dog the impression that the compulsion applied, a necessary measure in itself, does not emanate from oneself, it would be quite advantageous. If these types of punishment were given on the recall, the dog would become hopelessly hand-shy. A single experience of this kind would be enough to ruin sensitive animals.

It cannot be too often repeated that the reception given must always be a friendly one and that it must be particularly effusive after the dog has been alarmed. We must also keep in mind the second phase of enjoyment.

As devices for administering shock to attract attention at a distance, we have such things as the casting chain (a light chain about a foot long) and throwing stick. When using these one must invariably keep one's whole attention fixed on the dog, so as to be able to bring inducement to bear on him as required. One should not, for instance, be worrying about where the stick may fall, with a view to recovering it later.

As in ordinary backward run training, the dog is off the lead and at perfect liberty, while we keep our chain or stick handy, ready to throw. Open country only is used for this type of training. The dog must not be allowed to observe any preparations we make to use the device and his attention must by some means be diverted from his master, but he need not be in movement. The stick or chain should be used at a favourable opportunity, when the dog cannot see it.

At the instant when the missile strikes the dog or flies audibly past him or drops to the ground near him thereby causing alarm, the word 'Here' is uttered, caressingly during the first lessons, later in a sharper tone, and as soon as the dog, after his alarm, looks towards his master, the latter begins to run backwards, an attractive and extremely important procedure after administering alarm.

If the dog seems to be depressed, the previously described enthusiastic game is started directly after welcome. The dog is then again set at liberty. The long-range device should never be used on a dog as he approaches, but kept exclusively for the single purpose of causing him to do so. If the recall after alarm still leaves something to be desired, a mild form of compulsion only is employed, by resorting to the intimidation sound, a commanding 'Here', or the primary attractive inducements of the backward run, etc., may be reinforced as already described.

Particular care should be taken that exercises involving alarm are not performed in too rapid succession. Time intervals must be even longer than in ordinary backward run practice, so that the dog is given adequate time to regain his normal equanimity.

Exercises involving alarm are not only performed during specific expeditions with the dog but can also profitably take place whenever the dog, while off the lead, has been distracted from his master and is not at too great a distance for the employment of the long-range device.

The necessity of avoiding anything in the nature of a disagreeable experience for the dog on his arrival has been repeatedly stressed. This applies to all exercises performed when training is not yet so far advanced as to entail even a slight degree of fear due to compulsion. Before the application of discomfort after arrival a time interval is absolutely indispensable and is preferably occupied by a change of location and the provision of an agreeable experience. It should last from one to two minutes or longer in the case of sensitive dogs.

Here are some examples.

The warm welcome, and even more the enthusiastic game, results in the dog leaping joyfully up against his master and, frequently, licking him. This undesirable habit should only be very gently and gradually discouraged. It serves our purpose to be patient with it at first to avoid marring the enjoyment of arrival.

One should never forget to fondle the dog when putting him on the lead, if this action is taken after arrival.

It is expecting a very great deal of a dog-owner to insist on his giving a warm welcome to the dog throughout its life on every single occasion, even if the animal has previously misbehaved in some way. It may for instance have killed a chicken in a neighbour's garden. Yet even so the dog must positively be welcomed with fondling. Some people may find this incomprehensible. Are we to praise a dog and give him pleasure after he has committed so gross a crime? But such a view is, of course, totally wrong. Even if we do not take this view, it may be difficult to keep cool in such cases. It must be done, however, if we are to be fair to the dog and not to prejudice the object of training.

We can only induce a dog to regard a certain undesirable action as uncongenial if the objects that incited the action are made physically available to his eyes and sense of smell. In the case cited, the dead chicken, if it can be obtained, can be used for this purpose, so that the animal may be brought to regard the sight and scent of chickens as uncongenial.

After having been duly welcomed on his return, the dog is taken, on the lead, to the chicken. On the way he is not subjected to any disagreeable experience. It is the chicken, of course, that has to act as the bringer of discomfort. Not until the dog is close to and both sees and scents the chicken is he (while held on the shortened lead) given a few vigorous blows, accompanied by the repeated syllable 'Bah!'. He may also be buffeted about the ears by the chicken, while 'Bah!' is repeated. After this, the dog is led away from the chicken and should be fondled as soon as the dead bird is beyond the range of his observation. The procedure may be repeated immediately. As a result of his experience of unpleasantness in the presence of the chicken and pleasure in its absence, the bird becomes an object of repulsion to the dog.

At the advanced stage of training, when the dog can be relied on to come merely in response to the secondary inducements of call or whistle, we must remember that what the dog has learnt does not make a lasting impression on his memory. Just as with human beings, a lesson committed to memory, unless it is, like the alphabet, drummed into the mind from infancy, has to be repeated from time to time in order to be retained. Regular practice is therefore undertaken with working dogs, in which the lessons learnt are repeated.

It is not only a question, here, of training in the acquisition of bodily aptitudes. In the first place there are differences between learning intelligently and learning by heart. We may try to repeat, without looking at the paper, the seven numbers 2, 4, 8, 16, 32, 64, 128. We shall be able to do it at once if we can grasp the mathematical significance of this series of figures. But if we try to repeat the seven numbers 118, 9, 2, 7, 19, 3 and 26, we cannot do it. This series can only be learnt by heart. We are only able to learn the figures by frequent repetition and we only remember them if we again repeat them occasionally after they have been learnt. Otherwise the associations established dissolve; we forget. In the dog's case it is the same. The lessons we teach him are learnt on a basis of memory, not of intelligence.

A dog is trained to behave in a certain way and to do so in response to certain auditory or visual signals. Associations are established between these secondary inducements and the behaviour which the primary inducements bring about. The purpose of repetitions after the lesson has been learnt is to ensure that these associations do not relax or actually dissolve but remain fixed in the memory.

In other words, in order to obtain a fully trained dog the primary inducements must occasionally be used at the same time as the secondary ones. The former are, of course, as has several times been emphasized, the true renovating forces operative on the active and passive services required from the dog. Thus, in order to achieve a reliable recall, the backward run and, where necessary, the administration of alarm must, from time to time, be employed in combination with 'Here' or the whistle. So, too, must downward pressure be used in teaching the down, the jerk at the lead in heel work and so on.

When the dog fails to execute a movement already learnt, it does so not from disobedience but through forgetfulness, caused by lack of, or insufficient, training and repetition.

Finally, it should be realized that the following object of training may be envisaged as a service to be rendered by the working dog. The animal which comes to his handler at enhanced speed in response to call or whistle, is to take up a position of his own accord, on the man's left side if the latter is standing. If the man is walking the dog is likewise to come of its own accord to his left side and follow him. In neither case should the dog be allowed to move away until the auditory signal for release is given.

Two different auditory signals, call or whistle, are used in the recall exclusively. The whistle is only used because it carries further than the human voice.

Many trainers are in the habit of continually whistling to the dog, without thereby intending him to come close to them. This may happen, for example, when the dog is running ahead and we wish to indicate to the animal that we are turning a corner, going into a shop or something of that sort. One should make an irrevocable rule, that 'Here' must be recognized by the dog as a signal for attracting him immediately, under any circumstances, to close contact with his master. Whenever 'Here' is uttered, the dog must be made to come quite close up to his master and must, if possible, be fondled.

If it is not desired that the dog should come close in but the intention is only that the animal should notice what we are doing or observe the new direction that we are taking, the signal 'Here' should never be employed, but a new one, which may be called a warning signal, should be chosen for the purpose. Some kind of clicking of the tongue or a mouselike squeak would be best. The latter is made when one sucks in air with pursed lips. The dog will turn his head as soon as he hears this signal and instead of running to his handler will take the latter's new direction. If the same signal is employed whether the dog is to come close in or only look round and take note of his handler's direction, how can the animal understand the meaning of the word 'Here'? And yet, when a dog fails to understand he is called disobedient!

Special care is requiredn calling a dog when it meets another of the same sex. The progress of this sort of canine encounter will repay observation. We must remember that when two dogs of the same sex and about the same size meet they usually regard each other as enemies. If they are mature, both males and females scent a rival. They move stiffly towards and round each other, sniffing and ascertaining each other's sex, and eventually part with slow and stiff movements, only breaking into a faster gait when they are well apart. If one of them takes to flight before the encounter, he exposes himself to hostile pursuit. The only way to avoid this is to proceed with the encounter as described. If, therefore, we whistle to a dog so engaged, he cannot in such circumstances obey the summons, for he would at once be attacked by the other dog if he ran away. The encounter must proceed in the canine fashion. The dog summoned must actually, for his own sake, first part in slow motion from the other and only then move faster. If dogs are alarmed while encountering each other, a fight starts immediately, since the convulsive twitch induced by alarm is taken for the preliminary to an attack or flight.

In considering the main aspects of teaching the recall we must continually bear in mind the necessity for keeping both phases of the enjoyment in view.

In the first phase, that which covers the recall until the dog comes quite close, discomfort should only be applied in very rapid alternation with a pleasurable experience. A novice dog, or one being trained, which has made physical contact with the master must, without exception, be given a warm welcome. Even the trained animal should never experience the slightest discomfort while in this position. In the second phase a time interval must elapse, occupied by the agreeable experience and lasting from one to two minutes, before the dog is subjected to any less agreeable experience.

Not until the trainer has learnt how to allot pleasantness and unpleasantness as he would with children whom he controls, as they walk, by calling to them, will he satisfy one of the principal requirements for creating an understanding between man and dog.

This applies throughout the entire course of training.

CHAPTER VI

STANDING STILL—JUMPING

I. STANDING STILL

AUDITORY signal: 'Stay'. Visual signal: sudden presentation of the palm of the hand in front of the dog's eyes. Service requirement: when both signals are given together, or the auditory one alone, the dog is at once to stand still, and neither sit nor lie down. The duration of the posture will be determined by the

FIG. 8

Visual signal to stand still

object of training. (*See* Fig. 8.) This exercise is not performed in conjunction with heel work. The primary inducements to standing still begin by alarming the animal, and if this happened while it was doing heel work the dog would be rendered uneasy. This undesirable association is accordingly prevented. Standing still is taught without the dog expecting it, e.g. while the trainer is taking a rather long walk straight ahead, with the animal on the lead and it is pressing forward, possibly in anticipation of forthcoming man work. On such an occasion the trainer will suddenly stop, jerking the lead, thus bringing the dog to a standstill, saying at the same time in a commanding and long-drawn-out tone 'Stay' and presenting the palm of the right hand to the animal's nose. Immediately after these inducements the trainer will turn slowly round, by the left, so as to stand directly in front of the dog, facing it.

If the animal changes its attitude in any way, the trainer must at once catch hold of it. He then retires very slowly to a point at which he can still touch the dog at arm's length and induces the animal, by the means already described, to stand still, each time it attempts to move, uttering a simultaneous 'Stay' and making the prescribed hand movement. Repetitions of the exercise in rapid succession are only undertaken if the dog shows no sign of fear. It may try, several times, to sit or to lie. The trainer must then raise it with the palm of the hand till it stands up again.

The exercises are intensified by the trainer going farther and farther away from the dog, which is still on the lead. He will walk slowly away to begin with, keeping the dog under continuous observation and immediately applying compulsion, at long range, by a threatening 'Stay' or, at an advanced stage of training, by a flick at the lead, the moment the dog does not behave as desired.

As in the case of teaching the down, the sound of encouragement is not used when the dog behaves as desired. The maintenance of a submissive mood is as desirable in this exercise as in that of the down.

Training is intensified until the trainer moves out of the standing dog's line of vision and even out of range of its scent. But he must still keep the animal under continuous observation, so as to be able to intervene at once if necessary.

It will be a particular temptation for the dog to move if the trainer runs away quickly or throws himself to the ground or runs about at a distance. But the training must include these movements.

Finally, work is undertaken in the presence of distractions, e.g. in places where people and vehicles are passing and other dogs or similar disturbing factors are in the neighbourhood.

2. JUMPING
Auditory signal: 'Up, up'.

We are here concerned with long jumps over brooks and

ditches, high jumps over hedges and low lying obstacles, and scale jumps over walls and fences. The height of the latter prescribes the height of the scale jump. A dog may be able to attain considerably higher levels, but every owner or trainer should be too fond of his dog and value it too highly to subject it to dangerous exercises which would serve no practical purpose on active service.

The scale jump, which we shall treat first, imposes a quite exceptional strain on most dogs, particularly those with physical shortcomings or those which are not yet full grown. With the latter the scale jump should either not be taught at all or else be restricted at most to slight elevations. The ground from which the animal takes off and that on which it lands should always be soft. If training takes place in a room, thick mats are an absolutely necessity. Jumping should never be practised for very long. The best plan is to make the dog jump two or three times at the start and after the end of each day's training, or once or twice in the case of more considerable heights.

Far less resistance will be encountered if jumping practice is allotted as advised. If exercises last a long time the dog would not be able to see his advantage in continuing them, whereas he will recognize it at once if he is always left in peace after a few jumps.

Training can proceed, from the start, with the dog jumping forwards and backwards across the obstacle, uninterruptedly. The animal will soon get used to it and regularly execute the return jump of its own accord. A start may be made with a jump of one and a half feet and for some considerable time the dog must be kept on the lead, so that it remains under control and thus more amenable to compulsion. If at a later stage of training the animal is released from the lead and then refuses to take the jump, it must always be put on the lead again, till resistance to the exercise comes to an end. An easily adjustable jump is advisable in teaching this exercise.

One should get into the habit, from the start, of walking up to the jump and stepping over it. Otherwise the dog may well decline to make the necessary effort.

To begin with the trainer steps over the jump and as a rule the dog will follow him at once, clearing the obstacle with a high leap if it is a low one. The dog must immediately be induced to make the return jump in the same way. Each time the animal makes the leap the sound 'Up, up' is to be uttered. (*See* Fig. 9.)

Soon afterwards an attempt may be made to get the dog to jump without the trainer stepping over. A run is taken up to the jump with the dog to one's left, the signal being given just as one reaches it. If the dog refuses, the trainer must *immediately* step over the obstacle again.

The height of the jump must be increased very gradually. When it is high enough to prevent the trainer stepping over it, the dog is made to sit down a few paces away, or given to an assistant to hold, while the trainer walks round to the other side of the jump and utters the jumping call, with a simultaneous jerk at the lead. But one should never pull the dog right up to or over the jump with the lead. On the contrary, an effort should be made to get the animal to retire a little from the obstacle, so that he can take a run at it.

Whenever the dog refuses, we must find out whether it does so because it is overtired, has sustained some injury or is instinctively averse to an unfamiliar movement.

The skin between the toes of the forepaws is often exposed to injury and should be closely examined; if injuries are found, jumping should be stopped. If the dog is seen to be overtired, the jump is lowered and the exercise then renewed. The animal is thus rendered more submissive than if the training is broken off without further jumping. If resistance occurs, a few more attempts at inducement should be made by running at the obstacle with the dog on the lead and giving a really urgent shout of 'Up, up', at the right moment, or by going round to the other side of the jump as already described.

If, after a number of such attempts, the dog still refuses, the obstacle is lowered and jumping begun again. In all cases in which resistance has occurred but the dog has, nevertheless, by making an effort finally made the jump, even when lowered, the training is at once stopped, as this action will cause the dog to perceive clearly the advantage to be gained by jumping.

The taking of higher jumps by the dog on the auditory signal alone indicates that resistance has been overcome. He is then made to sit before jumping and not to get ready to jump till he hears the 'Up, up' call.

Retrieving over a jump does not begin until the dog has

FIG. 9
First jumping exercises

shown he enjoys jumping and has become reliable on the retrieve. A fresh start is made at quite a low level, say one and a half feet, which is gradually raised.

In this exercise the dog should never be made to carry a heavy dumb-bell, which is very bad for his jaws and, indeed, for his whole body.

CHAPTER VII

REFUSAL OF FOOD AND CURE OF THE HABITS OF EATING OR ROLLING IN REFUSE—RETRIEVING

1. REFUSAL

WE MAY never assume that the dog has any idea of the reason for the services we demand of him. Even if, for example, the dog has already learnt that eating in a particular environmental situation, as when tied up, is associated with pain, and he consequently avoids eating in such a situation, there still remain a number of gaps in his cerebral processes which have to be filled in by a similar experience. For, in addition to that of being tied up, there are many quite different environmental conditions in which the taking of food is not painful.

These conditions have to be introduced into the exercises, for every one of them represents a new exercise which has to be specially learnt by the dog.

In all such cases strict compulsion is required, as otherwise the intense satisfaction obtained in eating cannot be transformed into a disagreeable experience.

The most important of such conditions are as follows: Refusal of food already on the ground, in other words not recognizable by the dog as offered or thrown to him, and when he is either at liberty, ahead of his master, or at the latter's side, either on or off the lead. Next, refusal of food found by the dog while at liberty or offered or thrown to him in such circumstances, for example during reconnaissance, in the absence of his master, by a stranger. Again, refusal or rejection of food offered or thrown to the dog in its kennel or in strangers' houses. Finally, a similar situation when the animal is tied up.

The most difficult thing to do is to get the dog to refuse food anywhere and under any circumstances while he is at liberty. Even animal or human excrement as well as putrid meat, on which the dog enjoys rolling, must be included here. To cure a dog of this habit while he is at liberty is excessively difficult owing to the fact that the trainer is often not in a position to apply the requisite strict form of compulsion the moment the undesirable act occurs. As we know, even the strictest compulsion is of no use 'after the fact'.

Accordingly, we must be prepared, when taking the dog out off the lead, to keep him constantly in view, in order to be able to intervene at once when he seems about to pick up food or roll on it. Objects likely to entice the dog are placed beforehand on the route to be taken, which must be regularly changed. These exercises have to be repeated methodically and over and over again, to prevent the dog forgetting the disagreeable experience which ensues.

Good opportunities for breaking the habit will occur while other types of training are being carried out, if objects of enticement, such as raw and cooked meat, raw and smoked pieces of herring, the carcasses of small animals such as mice, or birds or frogs, dung and so on are scattered about the training-ground. These objects are not removed, but others are placed from time to time at different points of the ground.

After a time these objects decompose and represent a strong temptation to the dog to eat and roll in them. He should often be deliberately enticed to perform such undesirable acts, for this will be the quickest way to break him of the habit. Meanwhile the trainer must, of course, never cease to keep the animal under observation, so as to be able to intervene at the decisive moments.

When the dog is at liberty the inducement brought to bear is a loud and threatening 'Bah!'. If the casting chain or throwing stick is being used, it should be held in readiness and thrown at the dog at the decisive moment, with a simultaneous 'Bah!', the throw being applied in immediate connection with the recall of the animal (*see* page 92). When the chain or stick is used, followed immediately by recalling the dog, the objects of enticement, i.e. food and refuse, will in the course of training come to form a secondary inducement to the recall. The dog will then, as soon as he picks up the relative scent, come to the trainer of his own accord. This type of training, however, can only proceed if the recall thereby induced does not prejudice the purpose in view. If it does so, a different method must be employed. In cases where the loud and threatening 'Bah!' has no effect there is nothing for it but to take the dog at once, on the lead, to the objects of enticement and employ strict compulsion if the animal shows the least sign of being attracted by them. It will not be until the dog's inclination to these objects has been turned to disinclination that he will be set at liberty during training, always, of course, in different localities, and the sternly accentuated 'Bah!' uttered, if inclination again becomes evident. Should this secondary compulsive inducement be in vain, the dog must be made to approach by switching to an amiable attitude. One then pauses while the animal is again treated in friendly fashion, and not until then are the objects of enticement once more visited, with the dog on the lead, and a strict form of compulsion applied as soon as it becomes certain that the animal has noticed the scent.

In order to get the dog used to rejecting food in the neighbourhood of the kennel or in the house, similar preventive measures will at first be necessary. The animal should be given good and abundant food. He is always easier to manage in the kennel or in the house. The unchanging environment associated by the animal with the disagreeable experiences imposed upon him facilitates the result.

The dog should only be fed by his trainer and feeding should only take place at certain times of the day, at a certain place and from a certain dish. As soon as the animal has taken its food the dish should be removed, together with the fragments of the meal that remain in it or near it. It is a good plan to train the animal not to take food offered him by the trainer or anyone else, for instance at table, except at the usual place and from the usual dish.

As the dog must be taken on long expeditions and thus fed away from the kennel or house, he has to be trained only to take food at a certain sound of a secret nature. Both results can easily be achieved. Food is held out to the dog, and as soon as he snaps or only merely sniffs at it he is given a smart blow. This procedure is followed repeatedly and it is essential that it should occur at different places. If it is desired to train the animal to take food at a certain auditory signal, he is only fed after this has been uttered, previous inducements being given as described. Similarly he may be thrown something, the switch being held in readiness, unseen by the dog, for instant intervention if required. If the dog ceases to take food offered to him while the trainer is near, he is thrown a special tit-bit while in his kennel or, if he has been taken into the house, one is dropped beside his usual place or, if he is left down, at that point. The trainer then observes him from some hiding-place, without the animal suspecting his presence, for some considerable time. The primary rule must, however, always be that correction must instantly be imposed if the dog shows the least inclination to take the food.

Similar exercises should be undertaken with the help of a number of strangers, though the inducement to refuse food must only come from the trainer. If the dog ceases to take any interest in the food thrown to him, even if he is left alone for a long time, food is offered or thrown by a stranger when he is working at a distance from the trainer, for instance during reconnaissance, or the morsel may be laid on the trail.

It is easiest to induce the dog to abstain from food when he is tied up. Here, too, inducement to refuse food must come only from the trainer. He offers or throws food to the tied dog and applies strong correction if there is any sign of a desire to eat.

If the animal ceases to pick up food from the ground, the trainer retires, hides himself and observes the unsuspecting dog for longer and longer periods.

One should also remember to make frequent changes in the kind of objects used for enticement.

It must again be emphasized that in all cases where a certain environment, e.g. house or kennel, is not being used in teaching food refusal, locations must be varied, as must the way in which the animal is tied up if he is to be kept under such restraint. Otherwise certain stimuli from the environment will become associated with the act of refusal and if they are absent the dog will fail to respond to its previous training.

For example, if the dog during training is always fastened to a post by a chain, the reaction of the painful stimulus consisting in the refusal of food will become associated with the visual stimulus of the post and the chain, and the auditory stimulus provided by the latter. The dog may then decline the act of refusal if for once in a way he is not tied to a post or a lead is used to tie him instead of a chain. One must, therefore, dis-solve the association of the painful stimulus with the reaction of food-refusal, to prevent its being the only effective one, by varying the environmental stimuli. The latter then become less important and play no part in the association formed.

2. RETRIEVING

(a) General.

The house-dog which is allowed unlimited freedom will relapse into the wild state if it gets a chance. It will pursue animals that run from it, bite them viciously on overhauling them and kill its prey. It will even devour its victims if it is hungry and before doing so will often drag or carry them to a hiding-place. Dogs which have to find their food by hunting and which have young, may drag their prey, or some part of it, to feed their pups, as is the invariable practice of the wild dog.

Young dogs pursue their companions, in play, as if they were their prey and will do the same with inanimate objects such as a ball or a piece of wood that rolls away. They will snap at the living prey-image and engage in sham fights with it, or may seize the inanimate substitute and carry it off. We take advantage of this natural instinct in teaching a dog to retrieve, and also call the submissive and pack instincts to our aid.

The dog's acquisitive instinct operates on his own behalf and that of his kind when he is at liberty, but a trainer transforms a dog's natural behaviour to suit human purposes. The dog is required to bring his prey or prey-image always to the trainer and give it up to him. The animal must do so even with objects the smell, taste and weight of which are highly uncongenial to it. Since such extreme demands are made, a strict form of compulsion is indispensable if regular and reliable services are to be obtained. One cannot, of course, say for certain what degree of compulsion is necessary with an individual dog that is to be taught to retrieve, and sometimes strict compulsion is applied from the start. This course prevents our discovering whether the dog has any talent for the service required or not. Nothing is such a hindrance to an inexperienced trainer who is anxious to learn, as having to begin at once with strict compulsion. If anthropomorphic tendencies exist, bungling by the trainer results and the dog is caused unnecessary suffering. Retrieving, when practised as a game, is most educative for the human participant. Consequently, retrieving in play should always be the method employed by the novice trainer, and indeed in all cases where the object of training can be thereby achieved.

The observant trainer will discover that many dogs soon develop a very strong inclination to seize and bring objects if the exercise is made to resemble play. If it appears in the course of training that satisfactory progress is not being made towards the end in view, a stricter form of compulsion should be initiated. By that time both trainer and dog will have reached an advanced stage of learning. The trainer will be able to impose compulsion correctly and the dog, since it is working in an accustomed groove, will learn much more quickly to evade strict compulsion by doing what is required than it would if strict compulsion had been used from the start.

Those who try to teach retrieving as a game must be guided by the following principles. In this case the man does not confront the dog as a pack-leader; he is often not even a teacher, but a pupil. He behaves as would a pack-companion of the dog and, as such, attempts to stimulate the animal to act in the manner required. Man and dog, so to speak, become playmates playing with the same prey-image.

The trainer must first decide how the dog is to be put into the right mood for a game, this being an absolute necessity for the exercise in view. The mood required is dependent upon three factors, the first being the sense-stimuli provided by the trainer, the second that of the environment and the third the psychological condition to which the dog has been brought as the result of internal stimuli. The individual character of the dog also affects the situation and is dependent upon inheritance and past experience up to the time at which training in retrieving begins. The strength and duration of the playful mood will at first vary, and one must take due account of this. Later on the mood grows steadily more constant until at last it hardens into a fixed habit.

If one rushes up, with angry shouts, to a dog that is reverting to nature and is at the moment carrying a young hare in its jaws, the animal will run off and in so doing may drop the prey. The same thing often occurs in teaching the retrieve, though the dropping of the object at such a time is the last thing the trainer desires. The dog may be alarmed in some way, for instance by being unintentionally hurt or shouted at, and the mood that renders him willing to retrieve is gone. We must remember that in teaching the retrieve only inanimate prey-images are involved, and these are naturally abandoned when there is the least excuse for so doing, before the habit of seizing and bringing has been formed.

If compulsion is applied before this habit has been fixed, the inclination to fetch is weakened instead of being excited. The preliminary condition for the practice of retrieving in play is to avoid under any circumstances producing a sullen mood in the dog. He must take nothing but pleasure in the affair. He cannot do so if he does not completely trust the trainer.

An undisciplined animal cannot immediately be taught to retrieve. If a course of training is given under expert super-vision, such training may be begun on the third day. In the case of a single trainer working from a book, the retrieve should not be begun until the dog feels at home. The exercises should await the formation of the pack instinct in relation to the trainer and this only comes as confidence in, and dependence on, the new master grows. Training is best begun with the dog on the lead and should so continue until the flight instinct has completely ceased to operate. At this stage some slight habituation of the dog to fondling, the sound of encouragement, approach and the gesture of opening the jaws with the hand as described on page 111 is also desirable. This practice should be performed at intervals separated in time from other exercises, so as to avoid the formation of undesirable associations.

Teaching the retrieve may be begun with a dog that has had little training beforehand, since we may at first neglect to some extent such requirements as the sitting or standing of the dog close to the trainer, its abstention from engaging the prey-image until told to do so and its sitting down before giving up the object retrieved. These requirements should not be introduced until a later stage in order to avoid anything that involves compulsion, or has involved it in the past. Further remarks on this subject will be found in the next Section.

As regards environmental stimuli, the right mood for fetching cannot be induced in a training-room where exercises involving compulsion are or have been undertaken. The dog's recollections of the discomfort suffered there renders such a place wholly unsuitable. A room free from recollections of this kind will be satisfactory for starting the retrieve. It is, however, equally possible to make a start in the open, provided the place chosen is not one where distractions which may excite the dog more powerfully than the prey-images are likely to be present. The animal must be prevented from becoming aware of other dogs, cats or game of any kind, whether by sight, scent or hearing. We must always remember that retrieving only entails the seizure of *inanimate prey-images*. Training should take place quite apart from exercises which involve compulsion. If, for example, the down has just been performed in a certain place, the retrieve must proceed elsewhere and after a time interval during which the dog is encouraged, by being fondled and played with.

A dog learns to retrieve with the aid of some object congenial to him, for which purpose a small piece of wood or light wooden dumb-bell will be found appropriate. Other articles should not be used till a later stage of training.

Though all the stimuli proceeding from the trainer and from environment may have been taken into consideration, it does not necessarily follow that we shall immediately achieve our first aim, the seizure of the object in question. We have in most cases no comprehensive knowledge of the dog's past and cannot, therefore, tell what associations he may have formed and what events may evoke memories of previous experiences which are connected with discomfort. In consequence, the reason why a dog cannot be put into the right mood for retrieving often remains obscure.

Internal stimuli play a part here. For example, a dog which is suffering from thirst, hunger, fatigue or some other disability, or one that has just eaten a meal, will be difficult to influence.

The duration of training and the number of repetitions required depend on the individual dog. The exercise should be interrupted as soon as the animal can no longer be persuaded to execute the movement required. Even a slight application of compulsion may well prevent the return of the right mood for some considerable time.

One does not start by throwing the object. At first the trainer keeps it in his hand while trying to induce the dog to seize it and then give it up. Were the object thrown at this stage an untrained animal would dash after it, gnaw at it and play with it. He would also be very likely to try and run off with it, even if he were on the lead. It is advisable to prevent any such attempts from the start.

The result may be different when the retrieve is being taught to a dog that has already had some training in the recall. In these circumstances we may make the experiment of observing how the animal behaves when the object is thrown—at first for quite a short distance. If the dog picks it up at once and holds it in his jaws, and if there is no trouble with the recall, teaching the retrieve may be begun and gradually extended, with due discretion, as described in the following sections.

(b) *Retrieving Drill*.
Auditory signal: 'Fetch it'.

Service requirement: methodical performance of the following acts: From a sitting or standing posture at the left side of the trainer the dog, on receiving an auditory signal, is to run, if possible at a gallop, to the object thrown, seize it immediately, without trying to crush or worry it, and dash back by the shortest way, again, if possible, at a gallop, to the trainer. The animal is then to sit or otherwise place itself close to and facing the trainer, holding the object in its jaws, until the trainer, by an auditory signal, causes it to be given up.

The important point is that the dog is to be *allowed*, not *obliged*, to take the object in its jaws.

The primary inducements causing seizure of the dumb-bell proceed not only from the movements of the object but also from those of the trainer. We must execute rapid retreating movements to and fro, right in front of the dog and away from him. Our aim is to awaken the instinct of the chase in the animal by movements both of the dumb-bell and of ourselves, and thus arouse the desire to seize it.

The trainer himself acts like a dog at play; one which has got possession of prey his playmate would like to have. Every effort should be made, right from the start, to arrange for the dumb-bell to be seized as near as possible to the ground, so that the dog may get accustomed at an early stage to the subsequent situation in which the object is picked up from the ground. It

will not, however, usually be found possible to make a perfect
job of this at the beginning of training, as it is hardly feasible
to carry out the extremely lively movements which are at first
required if the dumb-bell is held in close proximity to the
ground.

Training proceeds as follows:
The dog snaps at the dumb-bell held in the trainer's hand.
The dumb-bell is brought from behind the trainer's back,
made to touch the dog's body and dance about before his eyes,

Fig. 10
Dog snaps at the dumb-bell

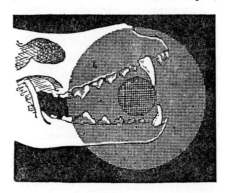

Fig. 11
Position of dumb-bell in jaws

then it is snatched away and hidden again. The dog's attention
has by this time been attracted. Then the game begins again.
The dumb-bell is rapped on the ground, struck against the
animal and rapidly withdrawn, while the trainer himself runs
a few paces away, encouraging the dog by 'There's a good boy'.
The dog then makes a leap but does not succeed in seizing the
dumb-bell (*see* Fig. 10). At that moment the dumb-bell is
thrust swiftly between his jaws, great care being taken to avoid
giving him any pain, while simultaneously a caressing 'Fetch it'
is uttered. The dumb-bell must not be pushed far into the jaws
but should be placed close behind the lower canines (*see* Fig.
11). If the animal has not opened his jaws wide enough, the
upper or lower jaw should be gently grasped with the left hand,
while the thumb and the middle finger are discreetly inserted
between the jaws to make them open. As soon as the dumb-bell

is in position between the jaws both fingers are removed, but the left hand should hold the under-jaw gently from below. The whole time the dumb-bell remains in position—a few moments will be enough—a *continuous*, caressing utterance of the words 'There's a good boy—fetch it' is maintained, while the right hand strokes the dog's head. If the animal tries to open its jaws, one must allow it to do so (as any form of compulsion would end the mood for fetching) and the dumb-bell taken in the right hand. Next, the dog is again stroked and the sound of encouragement repeated.

Further inducements are repeated in the same way. The dumb-bell is brought into action, the dog tries to get it and it is inserted in his jaws with a *caressing* 'Fetch it', then the left hand grasps the under-jaw gently, while at the same time the right hand strokes the head and the words 'There's a good boy—fetch it' are continuously uttered. The period during which the jaw is held is prolonged very gradually, so as to avoid any suggestion of compulsion.

Inducements for giving up the dumb-bell.

The first step forward is made when the dog takes the dumb-bell of its own accord, so that it need no longer be thrust into the jaws. If the trainer proceeds correctly the dog will soon try to retain the dumb-bell in its jaws. One should encourage the animal to do so but at the same time take the opportunity to initiate use of the primary inducement for giving up the dumb-bell. For this purpose the handhold already described is employed. But the thumb is now laid against the upper or lower lip of the animal, pressing it *gently* against the teeth, while the word 'Out' is uttered in a friendly way. If this does not produce the desired result, pressure should be increased to a corresponding extent, but always only gradually. If one is able to remove the dumb-bell from the jaws, the dog is stroked and the sound of encouragement is employed.

Even if the dog does not as yet retain the dumb-bell in its jaws without assistance, training is proceeded with, though the following exercise is then omitted.

Beginning of the inducement to sit while giving up the dumb-bell.

If the dog retains the dumb-bell in its jaws without assist-

Dog baying but not going in to attack 'criminal' with stick

C. M. Cooke

Dog baying but not attacking injured person while
handler approaches

ance until the word 'Out' is uttered, inducement to sit while giving up may begin. It is recommended that at the beginning of this inducement the left hand should take up its former auxiliary position by grasping the under-jaw, while the right hand presses down the dog's hindquarters and the word 'Sit' is uttered. This action is followed by the usual head-stroking, etc. If any trouble is experienced with sitting, this exercise should not be imposed while teaching the retrieve but should be carried out separately at a different time and place.

The taking up of the dumb-bell close to the ground.

The next step is gradually to accustom the dog to picking up the object from the ground. The dumb-bell is moved to and fro on the ground right in front of the standing animal, so that he is obliged to make a leap in order to reach the thing as it dodges about. But it is not dropped on the ground. It is kept in the hand as before, but attempts are now made to get the dog to seize it as near as possible to ground-level. *It will be necessary from time to time to thrust the article into the animal's jaws again.* Other inducements follow as before. As soon as the dog has made enough progress to be able to seize the object when it almost touches the ground, a first attempt may be made to let it drop.

It is to be observed in this connection that a dog much prefers to pick up an object that is *rolling away*. At this stage of training a motionless prey-image still exercises too slight a stimulus upon the animal.

The dog picks up the rolling dumb-bell from the ground.

The dumb-bell is allowed to drop from the trainer's hand at a moment when it is moving close to the ground and the dog is just snapping at it. It then rolls along the ground and the sound 'Fetch it', uttered in a caressing tone, further encourages the animal to pick it up. The sound in question has, of course, hitherto always been associated with being *allowed* to seize the object.

As soon as the dog has the dumb-bell in its jaws a primary inducement to recall is brought to bear by the trainer, as he, facing the dog, runs a few paces backwards while observing the other rules recommended in connection with the recall. If the

H

action gives any trouble, it is to be practised on its own account, as a special item, apart from retrieving exercises. As a rule the dog will approach without hesitation, in accordance with the habit already formed, and give up the object. The exercise is then concluded in the usual way.

The dog does not pick up the rolling dumb-bell.

We will now assume that the dog did not pick up the dumb-bell from the ground at either the first or the second attempt. He simply stood in front of it and stared at the motionless thing. In that case the trainer should immediately make a dash for it and put it into action again by kicking it or, as before, using his hand to start the business all over again. In order to increase the dog's desire to pick up the object, he may be held back by the collar for a few moments when he tries to make a leap for the article as it is thrown. If he shows signs of intending to pick it up, he is immediately encouraged by the words 'There's a good boy—fetch it'. If he still refuses, the whole series of actions must be repeated. The article will be pushed into his jaws with a 'Fetch it—there's a good boy', after which inducement concludes, as usual, with 'Sit', 'There's a good boy', 'Out' and 'There's a good boy'. The exercise is then interrupted.

It should be noted that whenever the dog does not pick up of its own accord on the attempt being renewed, the exercise is to end as described.

The dog picks up the article while it is not rolling. The dumb-bell is no longer moved about in front of the dog before being thrown.

Progress will be made when the dog picks up the object even after it has ceased moving on the ground, and a further step forward will be taken when the article does not have to be given any special movement before the dog's eyes but only need be thrown.

As already stated, even a slight form of compulsion will be sufficient to hold up progress several days. Training must, therefore, still proceed in the absence of any sort of discomfort for the dog.

A trainer who can acquire the least degree of influence over the dog will not have to wait long for success. He will find that need for preliminary movement of the object will steadily diminish. The inclination to retrieve the moment any indication of movement is shown will already have been formed. But there will constantly be intervals during which the dog's mood weakens; at such times the earlier actions must be renewed.

It is natural enough that for the time being the dog should pick up one day and refuse the next. Only gradually will it become an agreeable habit for him to pick up the object each time it is thrown. Until picking up occurs immediately after the throw no sort of compulsion should be imposed.

The dog lets the dumb-bell drop prematurely.

Special consideration must be given to the case of the dog which at an early stage drops the object which he has picked up before he sits, or before the trainer utters the word 'Out'. This occurrence may be avoided by gently grasping the under-jaw with the left hand. If the animal has already dropped the object prematurely, it is at once thrust back into the jaws with a 'Fetch it—there's a good boy'. Thus the practice will again end with an agreeable experience for the dog.

Application of firmer compulsion on premature dropping.

As training proceeds a firmer form of compulsion is applied when premature dropping takes place. The moment the object is prematurely dropped a sharp 'Fetch it' is uttered. It must be borne in mind that the way in which these words are pronounced represents a certain amount of compulsion. Consequently, the accent should be quite mild at first. Immediately after this 'Fetch it' the dumb-bell is very rapidly thrust into the jaws with a caressing 'Fetch it', instantly followed by the sound of encouragement, whereupon inducement concludes as before. If it is desired to use stricter compulsion to counteract premature dropping, such an exercise will be best carried out as a special item at a different time and place from retrieving, otherwise discomfort will be associated with retrieving and the right mood obliterated.

One should remember that the dog can only learn to retain the object in its jaws by finding that to drop it leads to discomfort, while to retain it leads to comfort. Consequently, discomfort should only be applied at the instant when the object is dropped, the latter being immediately afterwards put back in the jaws to the accompaniment of stroking, the sound of encouragement and 'Fetch it'.

Picking up the prematurely dropped dumb-bell.

The independent picking up by the dog of the object it has prematurely dropped is regarded by the animal as a process distinct from picking up the object when thrown by the trainer. The life given to the object by throwing it is in the former case lacking; it simply lies motionless before the dog. It can be restored to life by kicking it. If this is done, the words 'Fetch it' should be uttered at the same time. If the object has been dropped at some distance from the trainer, the desired action can often be induced by the trainer stepping backwards a few paces and simultaneously uttering the words 'Fetch it'. If the dog, in response to the harsh intonation now given to these words, shows the least sign of intending to seize the object, the sound of encouragement is instantly and repeatedly uttered. On the animal picking the article up a further 'There's a good boy' is immediately uttered. But if the dog refuses, a sharply accented 'Fetch it' is used the moment he desists. Immediately afterwards the dumb-bell is put back in his jaws with a caressing 'Fetch it', followed by the usual stroking of the head and the use of the sound of encouragement. The dog thus constantly finds that all discomfort ceases as soon as the object is in his jaws. If the inducements described have succeeded in causing the animal once to pick up a prematurely dropped object at the words 'Fetch it', the article is never again put into his jaws. He will always have to pick it up himself.

As soon as the dog is expert at picking up, carrying and retaining the dumb-bell, fast recall after picking up the object is taught, with the aid, of course, of the primary inducements noted in the Section on the recall.

Three undesirable associations.

Three undesirable and inevitable associations must now be eliminated. Hitherto one has always, on uttering the word 'Out', laid one's hand on the dumb-bell to remove it. This movement of the hand, as well as the sound 'Out', have therefore become associated with the reaction of opening the jaws. Thus the dog often lets the object drop at the very moment that the right hand is approaching the jaws to take the article out. The association is eliminated by frequently moving the hand towards the jaws without taking the dumb-bell away. The dog will then come to concentrate only on the word 'Out'.

The second undesirable association consists in the dog springing forward as soon as the dumb-bell is thrown. This action has been deliberately permitted in order not to disturb the animal's inclination to pick up. As soon as this inclination has become a habit, procedure is altered. The dog has to sit and is held by the collar while the object is thrown. The animal is then released. If he now tries to make a forward leap he is prevented from doing so by the appropriate inducement. He is not to leap forward until the words 'Fetch it' are uttered. Unless the trainer is well aware of the sense-stimuli he is producing, a fresh undesirable association may now be formed. Many trainers are in the habit of signalling the dog to retrieve by a wave of the hand. This gesture has the same effect as 'Fetch it'. As the trainer, in his ignorance of this fact, may at one time use the words 'Fetch it' before he waves his hand and at another wave his hand before he speaks, not regularly employing both at once, it will be impossible to form any stable association. Consequently, the dog will sometimes make its leap before the words 'Fetch it' and sometimes after.

As it is our purpose to get the animal to act only in response to the auditory signal, bodily movements should be progressively discarded in combination with the signal.

Method of applying strict compulsion.[1]

As was mentioned at the beginning of this Section, retrieving is not learnt voluntarily by all dogs. The reason is to be found partly in the individual character of a dog and partly in lack of appropriate inducement by the trainer. It may also be attributable to the fact that in training the animal a number of objects have to be used which the dog will take into his mouth only with the greatest reluctance, e.g. metals. The purpose of strict compulsion is to cause the dog to find that picking up and

---

[1] PUBLISHERS' NOTE: British trainers do not normally use this method as described, although in a much less severe form it is used by some successful trainers.

bringing in are more agreeable actions than refusal to do so. The animal must invariably be kept on the lead, so as to prevent flight. We are not concerned with punishing a refractory animal and compelling its obedience, but merely with facilitating the discovery just mentioned, which inevitably involves extreme discomfort. The abrupt alternation of discomfort with comfort is particularly important in this connection. The animal must be freed from compulsion the moment the desired behaviour commences.

Strict compulsion consists of two component parts: its operation is in the first place mechanical, when the dog's jaws are brought within snapping range of the object, and in the second place painful, causing the jaw to open by reflex action.

The dog, on the lead, wears a spiked collar, placed as close as possible to the shoulder, not forward towards the head, the spikes placed against the upper surface of the neck to the left (*see* Fig. 12). The following inducements must be applied in rapid succession as a single continuous treatment. The trainer seizes with his left hand the part of the collar on the right of the dog's neck (*see* Fig. 13). The dumb-bell is then laid on the ground about a foot in a diagonal direction from the dog's jaws. With a commanding 'Fetch it' and a swift thrust forward of the collar with the left hand (*see* Fig. 14) the dog's jaws are very quickly brought into snapping range of the dumb-bell and the spikes cause pain. The dog tries to defend itself by biting, and the trainer then presses the dog's open jaws against the centre-piece of the dumb-bell (*see* Fig. 15). The collar is now quickly loosened by being drawn back with the left hand. The dog's pain ceases, he closes his jaws and holds the dumb-bell between his teeth. At once the trainer's left hand grasps the under-jaw, holding the skin of the throat loosely, to prevent the dumb-bell being dropped and the head being disengaged (*see* Fig. 16). At the same time the words 'There's a good boy' are several times repeated in a very caressing tone while the dog's head is again and again stroked by the right hand. At first it will only be necessary for the dumb-bell to remain in the jaws for a few seconds. If the trainer does not get the dumb-bell between the dog's teeth in the manner described, it should be thrust, with a sharp 'Fetch it', into the jaws as they open, while the collar is contracted with a jerk. All discomfort then ceases again and an

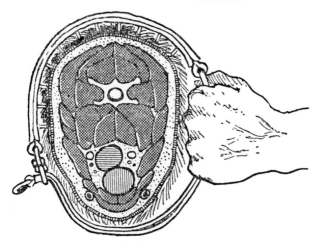

CONNECTIVE TISSUE & FAT

CERVICAL VERTEBRA WITH
VERTEBRAL DUCT & SPINAL CORD

MUSCLE

OESOPHAGUS (GULLET)

WINDPIPE

O ARTERIES }
⊚ VEINS } BLOOD VESSELS

SKIN AND HAIRS

FIG. 12

Transverse section of dog's neck according to Dr. Nitsch

agreeable experience at once ensues. If compulsion is correctly employed the dog will, after a few lessons, grip and pick up the object on his own.

If the dog tries to get rid of the dumb-bell or lets it drop after the left hand has been slowly withdrawn from the under-

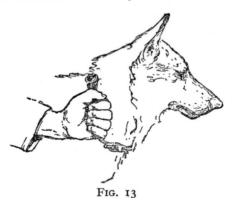

FIG. 13

First hold for retrieving under compulsion

FIG. 14

Second hold for retrieving under compulsion

jaw, a sharp 'Fetch it' is immediately uttered. Next follows, as rapidly as possible, the strict form of compulsion already described, involving picking up from the ground and inducing the animal to open its jaws, or, with the dog on the lead, the dumb-bell is held, with a stern 'Fetch it', in front of its jaws and placed in position by hand as the jaws open, as detailed in 'retrieving at play'. An agreeable experience must always be given as soon as the dumb-bell is held in the jaws. By this means the animal learns that dropping the dumb-bell means discomfort while carrying it means comfort, or, in the first stage of training, less discomfort.

If retention of the dumb-bell, as distinct from picking it up, entails difficulty, this may be taught on its own account at a different time and place. The dumb-bell is then placed in the jaws of the dog, and while it is on the lead and being fondled,

FIG. 15
Dog brought within snapping range of dumb-bell

FIG. 16
Grasping skin of throat and fondling

the under-jaw is held by hand and the animal is taken for a walk, at first cautiously and very slowly. Meanwhile the hand is discreetly withdrawn from the under-jaw to the sound of 'Fetch it'. If the dumb-bell is then dropped, inducement proceeds as described, but no compulsion is applied to induce the dog again to pick up the object. It is merely repeatedly thrust into the jaws accompanied by fondling, the under-jaw being grasped for a certain time. In this way reliability of retention in the jaws is gradually increased.

The success of the strict compulsion described above depends upon the trainer's dexterity. The whole series of actions must, as already emphasized, invariably take place at great speed and one should not be put off by initial failures. Since the dog receives, to begin with, a shock, his mood becomes one inhibitive of any kind of action. This situation, however, is soon overcome, for dogs are quick to learn and soon find out how they can evade compulsion.

As soon as the dog grips the object of his own accord, it will be possible to weaken progressively the primary inducements of bringing the animal to close quarters with the dumb-bell and the infliction of pain. In a short time the spiked collar will only have to be slightly contracted in order to cause the jaws to open. The next step will be merely to indicate such contraction. Finally, the sharp auditory signal alone need be used and the dog, while on the lead, can be compelled to pick up the object without primary inducements and without the trainer having to stoop to assist him. A contractile collar can always be used instead of a spiked one. Our ultimate aim is that the dog, at the signal 'Fetch it', should make a dash for the article, seize it and bring it at full speed to the trainer. Systematic training in this last exercise is undertaken with the dog on the lead as soon as he has ceased to drop the dumb-bell.

Intimidation of the dog is not practised at all after compulsion has succeeded; as a rule, it is unnecessary to use it again. Exercises are then performed without the lead. But one must resort to the lead and strict compulsion if the dog, in the presence of distractions or in teaching the retrieve with uncongenial objects that will be used on active service, refuses to act as desired.

After the retrieving lesson has been well learnt the next step is to teach the animal to bring different kinds of articles. The type of objects concerned will depend on the service the trainer requires. With a future police dog one would choose the kind of thing which people may lose, throw away or hide in open country—scraps of paper, paper wrappings, cigarette cartons, keys, jemmies, knives, revolvers, shreds or whole articles of clothing. One must also include heavy objects, such as parcels of clothing up to a weight of ten pounds, or rolled-up garments.

The articles must always bear traces of human scent, as the dog must get used to disregarding objects without it.

I should like to add one final word on strict compulsion in retrieving lessons.

No one, even the most sensitive, will repudiate the infliction of the pain necessary in such lessons if the following facts are taken into consideration. It is realized that human welfare and even human lives often depend on the reliability of the police dog. Moreover, the pain inflicted upon the dog by the methods here advocated is in its duration, intensity and application extraordinarily limited compared with that imposed in other methods of training which are based on anthropomorphic misconceptions.

CHAPTER VIII

DEFENCE WORK WITH THE GUARD DOG

1. General

OPINIONS differ as to the best methods of teaching man-work. This diversity is due partly to the variability of service requirements. If impetuosity were to become a habit with a police dog, the animal would be a danger to the police service.

The police dog used for escort service should not at first be trained to show hostility to strangers in the presence of his master but only to remain neutral. Hostility should not be shown until the handler utters a certain auditory signal. When the dog hears this he begins to observe strangers and takes up a hostile attitude if they make any hurried movement. He will oppose any attack or flight by the stranger by seizing him with his teeth.

These requirements will seem contradictory only to those who fail to understand canine aptitudes. Canine powers of apprehension, though very limited in comparison with those of a grown man, do enable the animal to act on the receipt of certain stimuli. While the handler is present strangers are not enemies at first. The auditory signal alters this pattern and produces in the dog a hostile attitude to strangers. The consequence is, not that the animal will bite, but that he will watch a stranger's movements and bark at him. This change in behaviour does not, of course, occur through the working of the dog's intelligence. His attitude is the result of events which have become connected with the auditory signal in previous exercises. A naturally friendly and good-humoured dog may thus be turned, in a trice, to a hostile one. This behaviour is indispensable in a police dog; it may also be appropriate in a mere house dog. But training alone is not enough; the dog's temperament must be right. Timid animals, for instance, are always suspicious and therefore hostile and prone to bite.

Methods of training the police dog and the house dog differ in the following way. The handler of a police dog has weapons that strike and shoot, while the householder is usually unarmed.

The latter's dog therefore is his only protection, apart from his own strength. Those who hold anthropomorphic views on 'brave' and 'cowardly' dogs may wish to have a dog with the attributes often shown in working trials. Here he may appear to be the 'bravest' animal in the world, not to be diverted from his purpose by the blows of a stick administered by a sham criminal in protective clothing, but ready to defend his master 'to the death'. The expert knows, however, that these heroes of the trial-ground may well prove useless bundles of nerves on active service. Their actual lack of interest in defence may in fact have been effaced by regular experience of fights involving no danger, and victories over a 'criminal' in protective clothing who is always the same man. It may be urged that this type of dog is clearly showing 'mettle' under test, since he does not flinch under blows from the stick. But, in fact, these blows excite just enough pain to stimulate highly the animal's resentment and resistance. It is possible to make even timid and sensitive dogs indifferent to the stick up to a certain point, for it should be remembered that resentment drastically lowers sensibility to pain. How will a dog which 'stands up to sticks and blows' get on with a real test? He will then be exposed to the greatest danger, for a real criminal will wield a heavy cudgel with all his strength. And a dog attacking a criminal armed in this way usually gets hurt and is unable to help its master.

This is the first reason why a service dog should be given training in a different type of defence. An absolutely necessary condition of his work is that when he is attacked with a stick *in the absence of his handler* he should not retaliate with his teeth but evade the blows and run round the assailant in a circle, or remain near him, barking. It is necessary to differentiate between the position of a householder and that of the service dog handler. The former is concerned with unconditional defence against the assault of a criminal who is perhaps threatening his life. Only in such a case could a very impetuous animal be of use. But the handler of a dog in the *public service* is called on to deal with different kinds of situations. His animal is required not only for defence against possible personal attacks, but is also employed to search tracts of open country for human beings or inanimate objects. Where the former are concerned it is important that the dog should *not* bite, but stand and bark. For this reason alone the training given to a service dog must be of a special kind. Innocent people may well be found in the district being searched. What would happen if a dog that 'stands sticks and blows' is hit by an innocent man out of fear? Apart from this, the service dog completely meets requirements, even in the case of dangerous criminals, if he merely evades the blows and circles round barking, *so long as the handler is still absent*. If the dog finds a harmless individual or an actual criminal in the district, it will fulfil its purpose if it stays near the man barking, but not biting and not retaliating. An innocent man will then remain where he is until the dog's handler arrives and as for the criminal, here, too, the primary requirement is that he should not be attacked by the animal, providing he submits quietly to arrest.

The criminal, once brought to bay, can then either stand still and submit to arrest, remaining unmolested by the animal, or attempt to evade arrest. If he takes to flight, the dog will seize him, if he attacks the animal, it will again start to circle round him or retreat step by step, avoiding any blows. In this way the dog will thwart the criminal's flight and the animal has fulfilled its purpose perfectly, for its armed handler is coming as fast as possible. On his arrival the criminal has two adversaries on his hands. The fact that the master is armed, combined with the dog's attitude, usually enables the arrest to take place without resistance. But if the criminal should then turn to attack the dog's master, the animal seizes the aggressor of its own accord, while if he attacks the dog the master is able to intervene, in his turn, without risk. Resort to blows or firearms is usually avoided in this way and arrest is ensured without risk to the handler. The animal has then fulfilled its second important task.

Training can never wholly exclude all risk to the handler, and one cannot count on security against even the slightest risks by having a dog which, in that magnificent phrase, 'stands up to blows and sticks'. Reasonable security can only be achieved by the type of training just described, which is indispensable in the service dog. Outside the service one can take any course one chooses. It is necessary, of course, to make sure just where one stands with the law if a dog oversteps the permitted limits in its actions.

Training for man-work may be undertaken, either exclusively with fictitious malefactors in ordinary clothing or with assistants in protective clothing.

The latter would certainly be inadequate training for the real thing, since the dog would be trained to pay attention mainly to the protective clothing, and would remain indifferent to persons in ordinary clothes. Consequently, when training is carried out in protective clothing, other people in ordinary clothes must also take part. They should not be used, however, until the dog has become expert at work with protectively clad 'criminals'. If this precaution is taken there will be no risk of persons in ordinary clothes being hurt when they join in the training. When the dog is trained for man-work without protective clothing it is, of course, exclusively concerned with people dressed as they would be in a real case, but great knowledge is needed before one can judge whether the dog which has behaved perfectly during training can be relied upon to act as required on active service.

The trainer should have a clear idea of his responsibility when he begins an exercise with an unprotected fictitious criminal and a dog which has not been thoroughly tested for absolute submissiveness—an indispensable quality for man-work. It might be thought that even the dog trained in subordination prior to man-work may prove insubordinate in the great excitement aroused by such work. It is this work, however, which teaches the animal a great part of the submissiveness it has to learn.

Protective clothing also offers advantages which should not be underrated. The dog can practise actual seizing from the start and the trainer is given the chance, whenever necessary, of bringing about the extremely important, immediate action of letting go.

The one-sided attitude at first taken by the dog with man-work in protective clothing does not entail any kind of disadvantage on active service if training has been properly carried out. One may compare the way in which reconnaissance for objects or 'seeking' is developed from the retrieving lesson. Retrieving, too, is at first learnt purely by rote. It takes place at a certain definite spot and is concerned with a single object, the dumb-bell, which is always thrown on these occasions so that the dog can see it clearly when it falls. It is not until retrieving by rote has been satisfactorily learnt that the transition is made to the retrieving of different kinds of objects and —in seeking—the use of the nose of the animal for finding objects which, because of their shape and colour, are not easily distinguishable from the ground. Just as the dog, when seeking, does not look for the dumb-bell, on which alone his attention had previously been concentrated, so with man-work he does not look for the man in protective clothing with whom his experience has so far been limited—not, that is, if the correct procedure has been followed in training.

Training of the kind now being considered should be governed by the following rules. *First*, when protective clothing— either a whole suit or padded sleeves—is worn, a spot should be chosen specifically for this exercise, and the assistant acting as criminal should not be changed. (An assistant who understands the results to be expected will enable the dog to make the most rapid progress.)

Secondly, in all training the fictitious criminal must be seen by the dog at the very beginning of the exercise. *Thirdly*, it will not be until complete control of the dog is assured in all possible circumstances connected with work in protective clothing that exercises without this clothing may begin, and it should never be carried out where the former work was done.

In later training both locations and assistants should be frequently changed.

Further details are given in the next chapter, on seeking.

It is a great advantage to begin man-work, with or without protective clothing, on the very first day of training. This procedure is particularly desirable with wholly untrained animals or with those newly taken over by the trainer and unknown to him.

Training will of course proceed, for so long as necessary, while the dog is on the lead.

Daily companionship between the trainer and his dog in aggressive action rapidly leads to the closest association of both within the 'pack'. The dog's confidence, dependence and submissiveness will then be won in no time. A further advantage will be that the dog's aggressive spirit will increase as the exercises go on. This will steadily reduce his depression, arising from the successive daily training in submissiveness, which, since it cannot be carried out without compulsion, must at first inevitably be independent of and separated from man-work.

The anthropomorphic conception that the dog must first of all be put through obedience exercises so that he may learn to behave 'to order', and that not until then will he be ready for man-work, is, as already stated, quite wrong.

The excitement and eagerness felt by the dog in the presence of the fictitious criminal enable the trainer to use the lead most effectively in inducing the animal to refrain from undesirable behaviour, and to bring it to a condition of absolute sub-missiveness. It is in man-work that the dog learns most rapidly when to bark or bay. Aggressive activity is, of course, itself the origin of the animal's impulse to do so.

The baying of the hunting dog, which was at one time taken as the stereotyped pattern for baying by the guard dog, comes into a different category. The hunting dog first learns to give tongue as described in Chapter IX, Section 3. The next step consists of displaying a deerskin in front of the dog each time he gives tongue at an auditory signal. After a good many repe-titions the skin comes to work as a secondary inducement, like the auditory signal. The habit developed in this way entirely by memory does not, of course, originate the impulse to bark, as happens in man-work, which naturally incites the animal to bark and bay.

The following essential requirements for man-work should be kept well in mind; only if the criminal takes to flight or resists *in the presence of the dog's master* should the animal be allowed to seize him. The dog should then do so of his own accord, without any prompting from the handler. The dog must im-mediately and spontaneously let go as soon as the malefactor's flight ends and his resistance ceases.

The dog must not seize the criminal in the absence of its trainer.

Training that merely makes a rogue-biter of a dog can never be sufficiently strongly condemned.

The dog's requisite determination in seizing can obviously never be induced by compulsion. The animal's pugnacity can only be brought out by experience in fighting by the methods described in the next Section.

Dog on reconnaissance finds a hidden 'criminal'

Leash tracking on a road

On the other hand, inducements must be provided so that the dog refrains from seizing and lets go whenever circumstances demand it. Compulsion is used for this purpose, since it is the only effectual way of controlling the dog's great excitement and suspense in man-work. Depression ensues at first but soon disappears if there is a clear separation between compulsion and its cessation. The excellent opportunity afforded by man-work for practice in submissiveness should not be missed. One final word: man-work should always be stopped immediately the dog shows fatigue.

2. SELF-DEFENCE OF DOG WHEN ALONE

No auditory signal.

The dog is more ready to defend itself against human beings in an environment it knows than in one it does not. He will be more resolute on familiar ground. His defensive instinct is also influenced by his distance from his trainer and by the time that he has been separated from him. The longer this is, the weaker his defensive instinct. A dog within the pack is more resolute than the animal alone. Yet the defensive instinct of a dog in strange surroundings and without its trainer is employed for a number of purposes. For example, a guard dog may bring a man to a standstill during reconnaissance before its handler can come up with the baying animal. The dog then, though left to itself, has to seize the man if he tries to get away and remain, even if attacked, close to him, baying.

As means to this end, training which promotes self-defence by the dog on strange ground, and without the trainer, will be useful. Apart from appropriate training in man-work, it will be helpful to accustom the animal to be left to itself in various strange surroundings. As this procedure can only be carried out by persons in ordinary clothing, the dog has to be on the lead.

For this purpose a stake is driven into the ground and the dog fastened to it with a strong chain (never a strap). The chain must be substantial enough to hold against the continual powerful jerks produced by the vigorous defensive movements of the animal and should be provided with a spring to take the strain imposed by the jerking. A further necessity is a special collar, strong in all its parts and about two inches wide. This will prevent the dog suffering pain as it lunges and pulls.

I

Training should never take place when the dog is left lying loose, nor when he is tied up by ordinary methods. There are two reasons for this. The first is that the usual equipment is not sufficiently resistant to pulling, and this may entail risk for the assistants. The second is to avoid such undesirable associations as might be formed when the dog, tied up with the usual equipment, anticipates strangers showing a hostile attitude and is led to molest innocent people. This contingency may be overcome by the special means described, which, by the rattling of the chain, cause a particular kind of stimulation. To make the distinction thoroughly clear to the dog, he should be frequently tied up in the usual way, care being always taken in the exercise then done, that he does not encounter people taking up a hostile attitude to him.

The exercises described below were at one time given the name of 'Object Guarding'. This title promises too much and makes the means an end in itself. A dog should not be made to lie, while off the lead, near an object for the purpose of guarding it. Such training necessarily makes the dog take up a hostile attitude to people who approach him and the object. Innocent persons who do so with no evil intent may then be endangered by the dog. For it is, of course, impossible to ensure that the animal will limit its hostility to growling, and warn off strangers without doing them any injury. Yet to put a tied-up dog to 'object guarding' would mean exposing the animal to danger, for a single blow with a stick, or the throwing of a heavy stone, might well render the animal incapable of defensive action.

The aim of training is to reinforce the dog's defensive instinct on active service in unfamiliar surroundings, and whether the handler is near or not the dog has to bay a cornered individual and if necessary seize him.

Defensive instinct cannot be reinforced by compulsion. This resource is also out of the question in work with a fictitious criminal. Nor can the primary inducements which provoke this instinct be given by the trainer. His part is played by the assistants and success depends solely upon their work.

The animal should begin to bark as soon as a stranger starts to approach it or attracts its attention. It should not, however, bark if the stranger merely passes quietly by at a certain distance or stands still looking at the dog. In order to achieve this it will be necessary for the assistants never to operate in protective clothing but always to be dressed in a normal, inconspicuous way. As soon as the dog's defensive instinct has been roused to the highest pitch by a single adroit assistant, he must leave the scene and the other assistants must be changed so frequently that the dog will not recognize them, even if the same man should be used twice. The ground for training should be constantly varied, to prevent the dog always adopting the same attitude in a known environment.

From the start the assistant must never show hostility directly he begins to approach the dog. Exercises should always be initiated with the assistant quietly walking past the dog for some time, out of stick range, and occasionally stopping to face towards or away from the animal. During these inducements any barking should always be repressed—of course only by the trainer in this case. The special collar and chain should frequently be used in tying the dog, in the absence of all the assistants, and the exercises should never be undertaken with the normal strap or collar.

To begin with, the trainer remains near the animal so that the dog's defensive instinct may be intensified. Fondling and sounds of encouragement are also a feature of these preliminary exercises. The auditory signal may be dropped as soon as the animal begins to act defensively.

The assistant's inducements take the form of his irritating the dog, mainly by being evasive and behaving as though he were afraid of the animal. Whenever the dog's defensive instinct flags the assistant should at once break off and run rapidly away in a straight line. He should stamp on the ground, run round the dog and dart to and fro in front of it, in such a way that the animal can pursue him, and frequently make sudden, swift backward movements. He should strike the ground with his stick and finally make off at a run.

As soon as the defensive instinct has been thoroughly roused, attacking movements are introduced, but if the animal's instinct flags at all attack should turn to flight. In this way the dog is led to feel that it has been victorious. Whenever the defensive instinct flags, the trainer encourages the dog, though never with the auditory signal 'Bark'.

The more the defensive instinct is roused, the more seemingly vigorous the assistant's attack should become. He should lunge, raise an arm to strike, with or without the stick, but should actually only strike near the dog, while uttering such sounds as 'Bah!', 'Stay', 'Get it', etc. If the dog gives ground or shows submissiveness to the assistant when he employs auditory signals, evasive movements must follow at once to stimulate the animal afresh.

When the dog's defensive instinct has reached a high pitch through these methods (owing to the lack of disagreeable experience) the exercise may be intensified as follows.

The trainer must gradually move farther and farther away from the dog until he eventually gets beyond the range of the animal's vision and scent. But he must keep the dog continually in sight. The farther off the trainer goes and the longer the period of separation, the less eagerness will the dog at first show in defence. The assistant must then return to his evasive movements and the trainer give encouragement from a distance.

Since on active service the dog may sometimes be enticed and not attacked physically, he must also be rendered proof against this method. For this purpose an assistant approaches the animal and starts off by making enticing movements. Directly the dog attacks with less than its usual vigour these movements are *instantly* replaced by the teasing gestures. The dog then learns, among other things, that enticement is a preliminary to teasing. The enticing treatment is now intensified, in the first place by protracting it and secondly by the assistant repeatedly uttering the dog's name in a caressing tone and making encouraging sounds. Special importance is attached to these exercises, as many dogs yield to protracted enticements, particularly when the trainer is absent.

Finally, it should be repeated that it is most important to change both the assistants used and the practice ground as often as possible.

3. MAN-WORK WITHOUT PROTECTIVE CLOTHING[1]

A fictitious criminal in ordinary inconspicuous clothes

[1] Training should be carried out in accordance with this Section or the next (4), but not both.

shows himself in the open, with no cover. He carries for defensive purposes a stick about two feet long and about as thick as one's thumb. It is provided with a thin leather loop at the handle, which is fastened round the wrist during work to prevent the stick slipping out of the hand, leaving the man defenceless against the dog. The stick is held close to the body, pointing downwards as the arm hangs relaxed. One must ensure from the start that the dog does not come to regard the stick as characteristic of an individual who is to be cornered and bayed. It should, therefore, be quite inconspicuous, both in the way it is held and in its colour. Nor should it ever be used in such a way that the dog is able to bite it.

The fictitious criminal himself stands motionless. The trainer, about fifteen yards distant, holds the dog on a short lead at his left side. The ten-yard leather lead used, the collar and its separate parts must all be of special strength to resist the heavy strain.

The primary inducement proceeds from the 'criminal'. He stimulates a hostile attitude in the dog by stamping on the ground, making short retreating movements and, if necessary, striking his boot with the stick, by a flick of the wrist—not by raising his arm. Meanwhile he utters abusive shouts.

As soon as these inducements have attracted the dog's attention to the 'criminal', the trainer gives the command 'At him' and at the same time makes rapid gestures with his arms in the direction of the 'criminal'. He may also, to begin with, run a few steps towards the man as a special further inducement. Many dogs will then make a hostile dash at the 'criminal'. If the dog does not do so the 'criminal' should intensify his inducements by walking or running backwards, at the same time striking the stick against the ground. As soon as the dog moves for the attack, the trainer lets the lead run through his left hand and follows the animal as long as it shows any timidity. The trainer should try not to diminish the space between himself and the dog more than may be required by the increase of the animal's defensive impulse or may be necessary for him to make the requisite inducements with the lead, which will be described shortly. A dog which is still advancing with some timidity will stop of its own accord a short way from the 'criminal'. One that is straining at the lead should only be given sufficient freedom to manœuvre beyond the range of the assistant's stick. The animal should never be allowed to jump up at the assistant or bite him, though one should try to make the dog bark. The inducement to bark comes from the 'criminal', while *to begin with* the trainer should prevent the dog jumping up at the man and biting him. The main point is that the 'criminal' should never use any stronger teasing inducement than will make the dog bark.

As soon as the dog barks, the assistant stands still again, his arm and stick dangling; but he renews the inducement directly the animal stops barking. By alternating action in this way prolonged barking, or baying, is caused, while no strong encouragement is given to the animal to bite.

Should the dog bark while on the lead near the 'criminal', the trainer stops any attempts at jumping and biting by jerking at the lead and exclaiming 'Bah!'. These inducements to bark and to refrain from biting last no longer than one minute. The trainer then retires with the dog and after a few minutes, at a different spot, engages in a repetition of submissive training. Cornering and baying exercises should not be resumed till an hour later and then in a different place and, if possible, with a different assistant. The changing of 'criminals' and environments as frequently as possible lessens the chances of the dog always reacting in the same way to a particular set of stimuli, the appearance and scent of one particular person and one particular environment.

As soon as the dog's timidity in face of the assistant has been overcome, the assistant acts as principal trainer and prevents jumping and biting. One of his objects is to make the dog stick-shy when the 'criminal' strikes at him *in the absence of the trainer*. For this purpose the dog has to be struck while in this state of stimulation. The force of the blows is made proportionate to the capacity shown by the dog; it has to be strong enough to suppress the impulse to bite in any circumstances. The point to remember is that the animal is to be rendered stick-shy, not 'steady under stick or blow' (*see* p. 152). On the other hand, one must not frighten the dog to such an extent that its impulse to corner and bay is obliterated. For this purpose avoid striking certain parts of the body, namely the head, forelegs, tail, hind-legs, and the abdomen, and to vary the force of the blows according to the individual dog. Each time the dog retreats under a blow, or several blows, the 'criminal' draws himself up and stands motionless, with hanging arms and the stick pressed to his body. To prevnt the dog's attention being drawn to the stick instead of to the man, the animal must never be allowed, as has already been emphasized, to bite the stick. Striking the dog's back, chest and hindquarters help to make the animal refrain from jumping and biting on the one hand and lead to the protraction of baying on the other. Attempts at jumping and biting are also countered by the trainer by jerks at the lead and the exclamation 'Bah!'.

When the dog has become fairly well used to baying near the 'criminal' without biting him, the trainer may drop the lead and let it drag on the ground. He must, however, always remain within reach of it, to pick it up if necessary. Complete freedom from the lead cannot be allowed at this stage of training.

The fictitious criminal works on the dog as before. If the lead is trailing on the ground, and the animal is free of the trainer, the dog often abandons the assistant after the initial cornering instead of remaining near him and baying. He must then intensify his inducements, making, in particular, movements of retreat. He may also run a few rapid steps backwards from the dog, with his face towards the animal. The trainer should simultaneously encourage the dog by the signal 'At him'. If this also fails, one must return for a time to work with the lead.

If the dog makes good progress, the distance between animal and trainer is gradually increased and the period of baying is slowly extended to as long as five minutes. At this stage the dog will be leaping round the assistant to avoid his stick. In this way the act of circling, barking, round the 'criminal' develops. As training continues to progress the assistant will assume a number of different attitudes. For example, he may lie or sit down and the trainer, meanwhile, keeps within the dog's sight. Training is carried on until the dog barks continuously even when the 'criminal' remains perfectly motionless. Occasional interruptions of the baying are countered by the assistant moving as described. By this means the dog gradually learns that when it stops barking the 'criminal' will make a teasing movement and prolonged baying will eventually be achieved.

If the dog bays for five minutes without any inducement from the assistant, and with the trainer fifty yards away, training proceeds so that the animal, though at first still fairly near the trainer, can neither see nor scent him. These exercises are very important, since they make the animal familiar wtih conditions on active service.

The *search of the 'criminal'*, which on active service often follows cornering and baying, should now be introduced. The dog must then, on the command 'Still', cease baying and stand at a stick's length from the cornered man. The dog must not change its attitude while the man is being searched, to enable this to be carried out without disturbance. Even if, during the separate submission exercises forming part of man-work, the dog has already been made to stand still simply on the command 'Still', the attractive force the 'hostile' assistant provides is so strong that it will at first be necessary to return to the primary inducements to make the dog stand motionless. For this reason the dog must remain on the lead during search exercises until it will stand near the criminal without making any mistake. The trainer holds the barking dog at the full stretch of the lead, then gives it an abrupt jerk and simultaneously utters a long-drawn and commanding 'Still'. From that moment the 'criminal' must always remain absolutely motionless. This exercise is repeated in quick succession until the dog stands still and ceases to bay whenever the lead is slackened. The trainer then calls 'Hands up!' to his assistant, who slowly obeys. The leather loop on the stick is kept round the wrist so that the stick hangs down from the 'criminal's' raised arm and is almost invisible. He then always has the stick ready for defence.

If the dog does what is required and ceases to bay, the trainer slowly approaches the assistant and the dog. He keeps the lead taut so that he can, if necessary, give it a sharp jerk by way of correction. On arrival, he takes the lead in his left hand, just behind the collar. Any attempt by the dog to move, bark or bite is countered by short, vigorous jerks at the lead and a sternly uttered 'Still'. Meanwhile the trainer searches the 'criminal' for about three minutes. The exercise should be repeated again and again until the dog keeps perfectly quiet while it is in progress. One need have no hesitation in administering strict compulsion, which can be applied without any ill effects, if the animal cannot be controlled in any other way. When the dog stands still and ceases barking on the word 'Still', training may proceed with the lead trailing until the animal does what is required. One should, however, return to work on the lead as often as seems necessary.

The 'criminal' has now to be taken into custody. This training is necessary to accustom the dog not to bite a cornered man when his movements are slow. On active service anyone cornered by a dog is told that the dog will be let loose if an attempt to escape is made. The talking required here must be imitated during training, for talking to the assistant starts a fresh set of stimuli and unless it is rehearsed beforehand many dogs will be likely to bite.

The 'criminal' goes off in whatever direction may be indicated by the trainer, who follows about five paces behind, picking up the trailing lead and holding it taut. In darkness the distance between trainer and assistant is reduced to two paces. The exercise should not be undertaken in the dark until work with the 'criminal' in daylight has proved thoroughly satisfactory. The assistant, on the orders of the trainer, may turn right or left and later cross streets where traffic is running, then enter a house and go upstairs into a room.

Attempts at flight by the 'criminal' should also be practised while he is being taken into custody. If the dog is not given this experience it will find that search of the cornered man is never followed by arrest and may, in consequence, abandon its hostile attitude and cease to protect its handler.

If the cornered man takes to flight, the dog has to pursue him, corner him again, bark and on active service, if necessary, seize him with its teeth. Attempts at flight are practised as follows.

The 'criminal', in sight of the dog, takes refuge behind a bush or other cover. The trainer immediately lets go of the lead. If the dog does not at once dash behind the bush of its own accord the trainer encourages the animal, running himself, calling 'At him' and using the visual signal. The trainer should, however, remain in the background as much as possible, but the distance between him and the dog should be reduced so that he can follow the animal and incite it to bay and stay close to the cornered man.

If, on cornering the 'criminal', the dog attempts to bite him, the man strikes the animal with his stick as already described. If the dog persists in trying to bite, the trainer counters such attempts from a distance by jerks at the lead and the sound 'Bah!'. If necessary, the animal must be pulled away vigorously.

Work with the trailing lead and, later on, with the dog completely loose, is not started until the animal is used to refraining from biting even when provoked by an attempt at flight. Standing still at the signal 'Still' is also practised during these 'flight' exercises. On the word 'Still', the assistant, as already stated, invariably ceases to move.

Exercises involving cornering and baying, search and arrest, with and without attempts at flight, should be performed in a regular sequence, so that the dog may become familiar with the various sets of stimuli as they may arise on active service. Training should also include the cornering of several criminals in standing, lying and sitting positions.

It frequently happens that the dog finds, corners and bays people who are subsequently proved to be harmless and may, therefore, be permitted to go their way. This contingency must also be rehearsed and always in connection with the down. The dog has to learn by practice that there will never be any struggle after he has been put down; the cornered man invariably going quietly away. The consequence will be that on the down the dog will cease to be subject to the tension which sets in when the animal stands still on the command 'Still', because of the exciting events then expected to ensue. To put it another way, the sound 'Still' signifies 'Stand still, refrain from barking, watch the cornered man', while the sound 'Stay' means 'Lie down, continue lying and cease to watch the man cornered'. The exercise is undertaken as soon as it is possible to work with the dog off the lead and the animal has already learnt to down at the sound 'Stay'. But in the present exercise the dog must be on the lead to begin with for, the hostile 'criminal' being present, it will at first be necessary to return to the primary inducements for the down. Strict compulsion may be used right from the start, without any undesirable consequences.

On the dog being put down the assistant is always allowed to move off at a quiet walk, every attempt of the dog to rise being repressed. Nothing teaches the animal to remain lying down so well as the regular experience that the down is never succeeded by any further excitement.

Attacks by the 'criminal' on the trainer are not desirable, as they would unduly stimulate the dog's impulse to bite. They would also promote continual restlessness while the man is being taken into custody. Defensive work with the fictitious criminal as described will arouse the animal's defensive instinct quite sufficiently to make it adequately perform the services required of a guard dog.

4. MAN-WORK IN PROTECTIVE CLOTHING

Command: 'At him'.

The assistant plays the part of a hostile assailant.

The 'criminal' stands in the open, perfectly visible, in a peaceful attitude, i.e. motionless, with hanging arms and the defensive stick held vertically in the right hand, close to the body and pointing downwards.

The trainer walks towards the 'criminal' in a casual and leisurely manner, with the dog at his left side on a long lead, which is, however, as in heel work, held short.

After the trainer and his assistant have conversed together quietly for one or two minutes, the assistant without warning takes the part of a hostile assailant. He smacks his stick rapidly against his protective suit or his boot, at the same time uttering menacing sounds and retreating steadily, at a walking pace, in a straight line with his face towards the dog. Alternatively, he may apply stronger inducements by striking a series of blows on the ground to right and left of the dog, moving steadily backwards as before. If the dog does not charge readily enough, flicks of the stick may also be directed at its forelegs, but only to the extent necessary to stimulate its impulse to attack.

In this exercise, as throughout man-work, the animal must not be given any opportunity of seizing the stick.

The trainer incites the dog at the moment of the 'criminal's' attack with fondling and encouragement (not the expression

'At him'), as well as by aggressive movements towards the assistant, while he simultaneously allows the dog to charge—though still holding the lead in such a way that should the animal attempt to seize the assistant it can be immediately restrained.

When the 'criminal' takes to flight the dog may seize him, but only if he still tries to escape.

As soon as the dog becomes exasperated and charges, the 'criminal' suddenly makes a sharp turn about and dashes off, keeping to a straight line. As he does so he takes the stick in his left hand and, raising his arm, holds the weapon high up close to his body.

If the intention is to train the dog to seize the right arm, this can be brought about as soon as the dog pursues without hesitation and seizes the man. In such a case the 'criminal', at the beginning of his flight, makes a series of abrupt, sideways movements with his raised right arm. Later on he lets it drop and simply makes the ordinary arm movements that accompany running.

If the dog shows hesitation in following the escaping 'criminal' and either does not seize him at all or only does so timidly, arm training should not be begun until the animal has overcome its nervousness. Before that stage the dog may be allowed to seize the man at any part of his body, but a high leap at the face or chest should be countered in the usual way.

The time taken to obtain the requisite degree of pugnacity and the requisite duration of animosity will vary according to the technical efficacy of the inducements used by the trainer and the 'criminal'. It will vary, too, with the aptitude of the individual dog. The age of the dog and its past experience will also affect the rate of learning.

The stage at which the exercises now to be described should begin depends upon whether the dog's fighting spirit has to be stimulated or lowered and upon the animal's progress in discipline.

At the commencement of the *escape* the trainer gives the dog a free rein and repeatedly utters the phrase 'There's a good boy', as they both pursue the escaping 'criminal'. The trainer keeps the lead loose, never allowing it to tighten, for otherwise the dog would at first become alarmed and its impulse to attack would depreciate accordingly.

If the dog hesitates in the pursuit and only seizes the man half-heartedly or not at all, the man merely runs another ten or twenty paces, then stops.

If the animal holds the man fast, only a few more steps are taken and flight then ceases.

The sound of encouragement is not used if the dog's pursuit and seizure leave nothing to be desired.

When flight ceases, the dog must immediately let the 'criminal' go and bay him just outside the range of the stick.

Cessation of flight may be defined as the abrupt end of the run and the simultaneous assumption of the 'peaceful attitude' already described. If, when this happens, the dog seems at a loss, the following steps should be taken to incite the animal to further action.

The 'criminal' turns *as he runs*, again teases the dog as already described and then immediately takes to flight once more. Alternatively, he may resume his teasing directly *after the cessation of flight* and only subsequently run off again. In this exercise, as throughout the teaching of man-work, there must never be any over-tiring of the dog.

If, when flight ceases, the dog does not instantly let the criminal go, it must be trained to do so at once. The trainer pulls the dog by means of tugs at the lead, away from the 'criminal' to beyond range of the stick, uttering the sound 'Bah!'. This action is immediately succeeded by the repeated call 'Bark, bark, bark'. The lead is then instantly allowed to run out, but the dog, as it plunges forward, is pulled back, with a further 'Bark, bark, bark'. This is repeated several times.

In this way it will be possible not only to induce immediate release after cessation of flight, but also the dog's spontaneous retreat beyond stick range and the initiation of baying; this last being necessary on active service, when during darkness or in broken country, for instance, it may be some time before the dog's handler comes up to the cornered criminal.

Important as it is to stress release by the dog, it does not matter much, to begin with, whether baying follows release or not. This development cannot be rushed. It will arise gradually from the experiences given to the dog during man-work at a later stage, when the animal will be brought into conflict with the 'criminal' in the absence of its master. Nevertheless, we may mention at this point certain inducements to effect baying of the 'criminal' and connected with the dog's release of him.

The object to be achieved is the creation and retention in the dog when flight ceases of a mood of expectation which powerfully excites the animal. No such attempt should be made on the casual cessation of man-work to be described later.

The way will already have been prepared for the mood of expectation by the 'criminal', directly after ceasing flight, exciting the dog and then resuming his flight. If the dog's hostility has been reinforced by repeated experiences of this kind, the dog need not be excited before renewed flight, and flight may be resumed immediately after its cessation, that is, while the 'criminal' is still in the 'peaceful attitude', the moment the dog shows signs of relaxing its hostility. On cessation of flight, however, inducements must always be applied by the trainer to effect release and baying as already described.

Alternatively, on cessation of flight, the 'criminal' may excite the dog as soon as it shows the slightest sign of being at a loss, in the following way. Without raising his right arm, he may strike his protective clothing or boot by flicking his wrist, at the same time stooping, as he faces the dog, and stamping vigorously. An abrupt retreat, while still looking towards the animal, will further stimulate its impulse to attack.

During these inducements the trainer stands by the 'criminal', holding the dog on a tight lead out of range of the stick and only lets the lead run out when the assistant assumes the 'peaceful attitude'. Then, if the dog plunges forward, the trainer uses the lead to keep the animal beyond range of the stick and cause barking.

In principle, the dog should never be more powerfully excited than may be necessary to achieve the behaviour required, and excitation should always stop as soon as the animal behaves as desired. Teasing should be renewed the moment the dog shows the slightest sign of relaxing. In this way the desired mood of expectation is soon brought about and at the same time progress is made towards the object of training: persistent barking at the cornered criminal.

Flight and release exercises are brought to a close by the trainer retiring, with the dog on the lead, from the assistant, who remains in the 'peaceful attitude'.

Taking the 'criminal' into custody.

Taking into custody may be initiated as soon as the dog has reached the stage of pursuing the escaping 'criminal' and resolutely seizing him, without it being necessary to tease the animal before flight takes place.

Baying need not yet be induced. In the approach of the trainer to the 'criminal', heel on lead in various directions is undertaken and from this point on inducements are applied to prevent the dog barking during the approach.

On contact being made with the 'criminal' the dog is made to lie down just out of stick range, to the right of, or behind, the assistant. As soon as the animal is lying silently and quietly the trainer has a brief interview with the 'criminal' and then takes up a position to his right or some paces behind him, while the dog remains lying down. Shortly afterwards the auditory signal 'Heel' is given, accompanied, if necessary, by a jerk of the lead.

As training proceeds, search of the 'criminal' may follow directly upon the down.

Flight or attacks by the 'criminal', representing exciting events following the down, should not be practised until a late stage of training and then only rarely, otherwise reliability on the down may be seriously prejudiced. When training ends, exciting experiences should *never* be allowed to follow the down.

Not until the dog's behaviour after the down is all that can be desired will the teaching of *taking into custody* begin.

The dog has to learn neither to bark nor to show signs of attacking, so long as the assistant walks quietly on and does not make any rapid movements. The animal should keep close to the trainer's left side, without deviation. The inducements required for this are as follows:

Firstly, since the dog is a far keener observer than man, he notices those bodily movements preceding flight which are made unconsciously immediately before running begins, but which may be so insignificant that the trainer does not notice them. The dog at once interprets them as the beginning of flight and, because of its previous experience, regards them as the signal for seizure. The experience deeply impressed in this way upon the animal's memory will be drastically disturbed if the trainer, who does not see these initial signs of flight, assumes that the dog is behaving undesirably and consequently applies a correction which is basically wrong.

To prevent such an error on the part of the trainer, the 'criminal' must be careful not to make introductory movements of the body and take to flight as abruptly as possible.

Secondly, the various exercises in connection with taking into custody must never begin until the dog has been escorting for at least twenty paces in exemplary fashion. During this process the sound of encouragement is not employed.

Thirdly, care must be taken not to practise the exercises regularly in the same order. This rule applies to all types of training where undesirable associations may be formed in consequence. For example, if during the process of taking into custody one says to the 'criminal', 'Off you go!' and he immediately takes to flight, the sound 'off you go' will come to be interpreted by the dog as a signal to seize.

Exercises in connection with taking into custody.

The flight from the dog is at first made straight ahead, followed by cessation of flight and the ensuing inducements, ending with the resumption of custody. If the dog works satisfactorily in this exercise, flight to one side or to the rear is attempted.

Next, the dog must experience attacks by the 'criminal', while in custody, on the trainer. As a preliminary, the assistant secretly takes the stick in his left hand. He turns to the trainer suddenly and rapidly, lifting his left arm quickly, as if to strike, stab, or shoot. If, when this attack takes place, the dog does not instantly seize the 'criminal', the trainer lets himself be pushed back in a straight line, so that, from the dog's point of view, the adversary is giving ground before it and the animal's instinct to attack is therefore stimulated.

The 'criminal's' attack, which may be practised in various forms during taking into custody, ends abruptly with his

assumption of the 'peaceful attitude' and subsequent inducements by the trainer as required.

An exercise involving the fall of the assistant must also be
practised, both before he is caught and seized by the dog and
during actual seizure. The trainer then applies the inducements
for immediate release, while the assistant remains quietly lying
on the ground. The man then slowly rises, no exciting experience
being allowed to affect the dog directly after this action.

Each time a man-work practice is concluded, the dog is
made to down just beyond the range of the assistant's stick,
while the 'criminal' maintains the 'peaceful attitude'.

One takes advantage of this opportunity as early as possible
to release the dog from the lead. The trainer slowly retires from
the dog, as it remains down, at first going only a few paces. He
stands still and shortly afterwards calls the animal. Then, with
the dog either on or off the lead, he walks away from the
assistant, who preserves the 'peaceful attitude' for some time,
so as not to excite the animal.

The repetition of this series of experiences: lying down,
being called, leaving the 'criminal' while he maintains the
'peaceful attitude', eliminates the dog's mood of expectation
which was formerly required but in the present case is not. It
also renders it easier to call the dog away after it has been
lying down, or even to call it away without previously making
it down, an exercise which has to be practised later on.

Here is a further suggestion about how frequently the
'criminal' should take to flight or attack during taking into
custody. The general rule is that whenever the dog's vigilance
in relation to the 'criminal' relaxes at all, the animal must
promptly be provided with an exciting experience. On the other
hand, the period of taking into custody must steadily increase
in length to make it more realistic.

*Cornering and baying a visible assistant on the auditory signal
'At him'.*

It was laid down in detail in the first part of this chapter
that in the presence of the trainer the dog should seize the
'criminal' when he attacks or resists, but not in the trainer's
absence unless flight takes place. The corresponding discovery
by the dog that it is never defeated while the trainer is present,

K

stimulates its impulse to attack to such an extent that on these occasions he seizes practically blindfold. When, therefore, as training goes on, the dog frequently confronts the 'criminal' alone, our second requirement has to be met: that in this situation the dog should *not* seize the 'criminal' who attacks it, still less if the assistant is preserving the 'peaceful attitude'. This is met by lowering the dog's degree of fearlessness, when left to itself, to the extent that it feels defeated and loses the impulse to seize the 'criminal' when he is not in flight. The means to this end are provided by blows from the assistant's stick.

Some dogs, it is true, retain their fearlessness even in the trainer's absence. In this case the trainer alone should operate if mistakes are made. As a rule, however, the dog's impulse to attack at once begins to wane when the distance between the animal and the trainer increases and as the period of separation lengthens.

With regard to the *cornering* of the 'criminal', the following exercises may be begun as soon as the dog develops a prolonged hostility towards the protectively clothed assistant, provided the animal has received a fairly comprehensive grounding in discipline. Regular work on the long lead and strict compulsion soon bring this about.

On the words 'At him', which are used for the first time in cornering, the dog runs up to the assistant, who stands in the open, and bays him, out of range of the stick, without showing any inclination to seize.

Until the dog is used to this, training is only undertaken at short distances of about fifteen to twenty paces, and a return is made to these distances when the animal's performance leaves anything to be desired.

The trainer approaches to within fifteen to twenty paces of the 'criminal', who is standing in the 'peaceful attitude'. The trainer then makes the dog sit near him, or stand at his heels. Any attempt by the dog to run up to the assistant before 'At him' is uttered is repressed.

On the sound 'At him' the trainer runs forward a few steps, making the lead long and saying 'There's a good boy'. He comes to a halt as soon as the dog sets off towards the 'criminal'. If necessary, the latter uses the attractive type of inducement, uttering menacing sounds, striking the ground with his stick and at the same time retreating. Such inducements are, however, given up at once, and the assistant assumes the 'peaceful attitude', the moment the animal charges him. If baying takes place beyond range of the stick, no inducements ensue.

If the dog does not bay, or if baying slackens, or the animal shows too little hostility, it is teased by the 'criminal', as described earlier on.

If the dog comes within range of the stick, he is given a blow across the back, chest or hindquarters. The force of these blows must prevent the dog's hostility from weakening but at the same time teach him to avoid them and to keep out of range of the stick. These blows follow immediately upon the 'peaceful attitude' and are given in rapid succession if necessary. The assistant straightens up directly afterwards and resumes his former attitude, but at once uses the stick again if the dog comes too near.

The trainer encourages the dog, if it is half-hearted, from a distance. If the animal shows pugnacity, only the assistant provides inducement. It is only when the 'criminal' cannot keep the dog off, despite the blows he gives, that the trainer intervenes from a distance with 'Bah!' and jerks at the lead. To begin with, inducements to leave go and only bark last one or two minutes, after which the following exercises may be added.

Firstly, the trainer, holding the lead short, approaches the assistant. The nearer he gets to him the more the dog's impulse to attack is stimulated. At about five paces from the 'criminal' the trainer must apply inducement and at the same moment the assistant assumes the 'peaceful attitude'. Then comes taking into custody, with or without a previous down, followed by departure from the 'criminal' when the final lesson concludes.

Secondly, after inducements have been applied by the 'criminal' to the dog set on him at the sound 'At him', the trainer attempts from a distance to make the animal down, doing this when the assistant has assumed the 'peaceful attitude'. As soon as the trainer calls 'Stay'—a simultaneous jerk at the lead will be helpful here—the 'criminal' must assume or maintain the 'peaceful attitude' and all inducements are then applied by the trainer.

If the trainer does not succeed in making the dog down from a distance, he approaches, holding the lead short, near enough to the assistant to put the dog down, during which the dog should remain perfectly silent.

In these exercises inducements to down ought not immediately to succeed the meeting of dog and 'criminal'. For then the dog would in time lie down of its own accord on arrival before the cornered man, instead of baying, having formed an undesirable association. If the down is obeyed from a distance, it is followed by calling off or by another exercise.

Calling off the baying dog, without previously dropping him, can also now be taught, provided the 'criminal' assumes the 'peaceful attitude'.

Thirdly, after the dog has been sent forward to corner and bay the assistant, with the trainer ten or fifteen paces away, the 'criminal' suddenly darts off in a straight line, whereupon the trainer lets the lead out, calling out repeatedly 'There's a good boy'. The dog, left to itself, will as a rule pursue and seize without the impetuosity and resolution it would have in the trainer's presence.

There is nothing to worry about if during the first lessons the dog pursues with hesitation and does not seize the man. To increase the animal's impulse to attack, the trainer may, in addition to making sounds of encouragement, run after the escaping 'criminal' and reduce the distance between himself and the dog. If this is not effective, the trainer may catch up the assistant, who turns and attacks him. At this point the exercise may be repeated or some other lesson initiated.

Exercises with the assistant in the absence of the trainer are a great help in preventing the dog from seizing the man it has cornered. They also facilitate training in prolonging baying.

The following procedure is adopted when the assistant is unable to attract the dog to the extent required in the absence of the trainer. At the start of the exercise the distance between 'criminal' and trainer is shortened. The moment the trainer calls 'At him' he runs forward with the dog and the assistant regulates his flight so that the animal is able to seize its man at once. This exercise, however, should only be undertaken in the case of really lackadaisical dogs, for otherwise the object of training would be prejudiced by reinforcing the dog's tendency to seize those who are to be cornered even when they stand quite still.

Training off the lead.

Work off the lead is started either with calling off after the down or with direct calling off from the 'criminal' at the end of each exercise.

A test is first made of the behaviour of the dog, while off the lead, during taking into custody. If the animal does not remain at heel, the lesson is at once interrupted. Both 'criminal' and trainer come to a halt and the trainer recalls the dog with the word 'Heel'. If the animal continues to misbehave during taking into custody, it must be put on the lead and the necessary inducements of strict compulsion applied. This is also required when trouble ensues in other man-work when the dog is off the lead.

It is important, when working with a dog off the lead, not only to bear in mind the system outlined in the present chapter, but also to ensure perfect performance by the dog of the recall and, in particular, of the down. These exercises are, therefore, specially recommended for study.

Exercises which improve man-work.

Hitherto the dog has only been attacked by the 'criminal' in the trainer's absence, through being teased and frightened out of any attempt to seize by the stick.

The dog now has to undergo the further experience of being attacked, when by itself, far more vigorously by the 'criminal'. In this case he walks or runs up to the animal and strikes it with the stick whenever it comes within range. The object of training here is to ensure that instead of running away from a man intent on attack, the dog circles round him baying or remains baying near him out of stick range thus preventing the flight of the 'criminal'.

The dog is set on the 'criminal' standing no more than ten or fifteen paces away. The trainer stands at an equal distance from the animal. After the dog has been baying for some time the 'criminal' suddenly walks, or at a later stage of training runs, menacingly up to the dog, but immediately goes straight on and runs away from the dog. As soon as he has passed the animal, the trainer, in order to encourage the now permissible action of seizing, calls out 'There's a good boy', repeating the phrase as often as necessary. If the dog hesitates at this lesson the trainer runs up to the 'criminal' who then attacks him thus reviving the animal's impulse to attack. The exercise may be intensified by the 'criminal' tackling the dog, after cornering and baying have taken place, in such a way that he remains continuously facing the animal, thus moving round in a circle. If the dog shows the slightest uneasiness at this type of aggression the 'criminal' turns round and runs away in a straight line, whereupon the dog repeatedly hears the sound of encouragement from the trainer. The point is, that so long as the assistant faces the dog, the animal is not to seize him but stay near him baying, out of stick range.

The exercise in which the 'criminal' attacks the dog before the animal reaches him after the signal 'At him' may also, occasionally, be practised. If the dog has behaved timidly, it should be given several opportunities to make a resolute seizure at the close of the exercises.

Training with assistants not in protective clothing.

These lessons may begin as soon as the dog has proved thoroughly reliable in man-work with protective clothing.

On the words 'At him' the dog, without any further inducement, must corner the 'criminal', but not attack him if he remains quiet, and bay him out of range of the stick for about five minutes, even though the trainer may be about fifty yards away.

Without any inducement the dog must also seize the 'criminal' whenever he tries to escape or attacks the trainer, and must release him again when he remains still of his own accord.

This will be the first time the dog learns to behave in the same way when cornering persons in ordinary clothing as when confronting the protectively clothed 'criminal' on the training ground. Training with assistants in ordinary clothing is indispensable, since it serves to train the animal directly for active service. These lessons are never held on the training ground and the locality, as well as the assistants, must be frequently changed. Until the dog has become expert the assistants must be fully familiar with all the inducements, which will still be necessary.

A 'criminal', equipped with the stick, stands in the 'peaceful attitude' in open country, where the dog can see him, having at first, as a precautionary measure, some form of cover, a tree for instance, behind him. If it is later intended to train for reconnaissance (see Chapter IX), trainer and dog must always be to one side of the 'criminal', generally about ten paces away. The dog, which is at first held on the lead, is sent off on the words 'At him', the trainer at the same time running sideways to corner the man.

The sight and also the smell of the 'criminal' will at first be unfamiliar to the dog, so that it will not, as a rule, behave exactly in the same way as before. Both trainer and assistant must, therefore, at first employ the same inducements as were applied to the dog when it was starting work with the protectively clothed assistant—particularly during cornering and baying. If this is done the dog will soon get back into the former routine.

When flight takes place during taking into custody, the trainer runs with the dog, holding the lead in such a way as to prevent the animal from seizing. This is about as near as one can get to active service, and the inducements used by assistant and trainer are sufficient to take the dog to the stage of training necessary for the real thing.

The cornering and baying of persons in the lying or seated positions, alone or in groups, may now also be undertaken, as well as the baying of persons in buildings or in darkness, including women. In reconnaissance children may also be used.

If training has hitherto proceeded as indicated, the sound 'At him' will cause a fully trained animal to run up to the person to be cornered and bay him, without doing him any harm provided he remains quiet.

This effect of the 'At him' signal is also important in all cases of unresisted arrest at close quarters. The sound 'At him' alone will then be sufficient to make the animal adopt the required attitude. From that instant the dog will watch every movement of the person in question and secure its master against any surprise attack.

As soon as the dog has completed its course with 'criminals' in ordinary clothing, it is ready to learn reconnaissance. Man-work in protective or ordinary clothing should continue to be practised from time to time.

5. So-called Stick-sureness

Unless we provide dogs with armour, we should never train them to be steady under the stick, for a single well-directed blow will always be enough to render them incapable of self-defence. A dog with its limbs broken can be of no further use to its master. In trials, steadiness under the stick is only shown under conditions in which the stick used and the force of the blows are calculated to spare the dog's bones. This may result in his attacking blindly on active service and thereby cause him to run into trouble.

On such a dog it may be said, "Well, he did his duty." But has the animal in reality performed any service to its master when it is struck down by the cudgel of a man it has attacked before being able to seize him? The only result is that the master is deprived of his dog's assistance. It is surely far more to the purpose so to train the animal that it will evade the blows of a man laying about him with a cudgel by merely circling round him barking or remaining barking near him. Surely the dog would have done all that is required had he brought the man who has to be arrested to a standstill and then cornered him? A dog trained in this way will seize the man in question should he attack its master with a stick, thus providing the latter with far more valuable service than the so-called 'stick-steady' animal. We must also be quite clear on the point that the dog's inclination to bite is so heightened by practice of the so-called 'steadiness under the stick' that an animal thus trained will be liable to become more of a liability than an asset through its biting tendencies.

Although we have stated earlier that the dog must be protected from the effects of careless blows, so that he may attack an assailant unhesitatingly when the real test comes, this does not mean that the animal must never be hurt. One may and should increase the weight of blows up to a certain point during the course of training. But the object of training will not be to render the dog indifferent to blows with a stick, but, on the contrary, to teach him to have a wholesome respect for them. Let us make the point perfectly clear by saying that *the dog must remain stick-shy in the absence of the trainer.* The force of blows during training should be sufficient to bring this about. Some dogs, however, are so tough that their pugnacity is positively augmented by the heaviest blows that their bones can withstand. In the case of such animals the impulse to seize cannot be weakened to the desired extent. To prevent them from biting anyone standing on the defensive the trainer himself must apply inducements of the most strictly compulsive character.

CHAPTER IX

RECONNAISSANCE AND TRACKING

1. RECONNAISSANCE
(a) *General.*
RECONNAISSANCE of human beings by a guard dog is based
on previous man-work. In these exercises the dog has learnt
that the auditory signal 'At him' is followed by exciting encounters with hostile people. Such persons were always clearly
visible, even in flight, so that there was never any question of
tracking them. Reconnaissance is built up on this basis. In
teaching it the dog is never given the opportunity to initiate
tracking; the 'criminals' being now invisible and, therefore, to
be detected. This is brought about by working the dog under
conditions in which finding is only possible through body-
scent. For this purpose the 'criminals' do not actually cross the
country chosen for reconnaissance, but approach their hiding-
places from beyond it. As soon as the dog has become familiar
in this way with picking up by body-scent, training is transferred to a place where many tracks, so far as possible of
equal age, cross one another in all directions, so that the dog
is repeatedly prevented from picking up an individual track.
It often happens on active service that the ground to be
searched has several tracks, and the dog is impeded in its work.
This tendency is counteracted by suitable exercises on ground
free from tracks or crossed by a number of them in different
directions.

Seeking objects, on the other hand, is based on the retrieve.
When the dog was being taught to retrieve, it saw the object
fall, so that the question of tracking never arose. The finding
of hidden objects is, therefore, taught in the same way as
reconnaissance of human beings. Further details are given in
Section (c).

(b) *Human reconnaissance.*
Auditory and visual signals are the same as in other man-
work.

We begin, during initial training, with a sector at least a hundred yards wide and two hundred yards deep. The entire field must be open to view and free from tracks. So that the dog can cover the whole length (fifty yards) of each arm of the zigzag, the directions should go with the wind until the animal has become expert. Unless this precaution is taken the dog will pick up the body-scent of the 'criminals' long before he has covered the fifty-yard distance. This contingency has to be avoided with the novice dog, otherwise the instinct to cover the whole distance of fifty yards will be obliterated.

An assistant, wearing ordinary clothing, is posted or lies down, under cover, at each side of the boundary of the reconnaissance field. (*See* Fig. 17.) They do not reach these positions by crossing the ground, but from outside it. The dog must not be allowed to see any of these preparations.

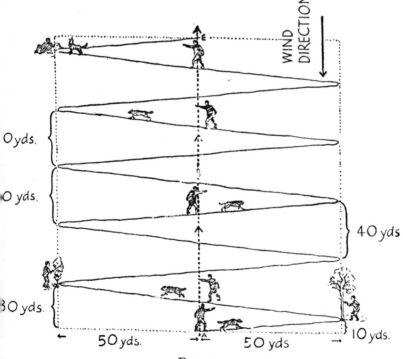

FIG. 17

Reconnaissance. A—E = handler's direction

Training is begun with the dog off the lead. The animal has hitherto been accustomed, on the words 'At him', to see persons standing or in flight at distances up to fifty yards. This visual stimulus is now absent when the signal 'At him', accompanied by simultaneous bodily movements by the trainer, is given. During the first exercises the 'criminal', invisible in his hiding-place, calls attention to himself by making a noise. As soon as the dog hears him the trainer makes the auditory and visual signals, at the same time running a few steps sideways to the right, in the direction of the sound. In this way the dog will rapidly come to recall the familiar events that formerly followed these signals. He will, therefore, run towards the noises, which are repeated by the assistant if the animal does not immediately run forward. The man having been found in this way, the dog will, as before, corner and bay him.

Attention must be paid to teaching the dog to quarter the ground thoroughly. He is to search the sector by a zigzag course running fifty yards to the right and then fifty yards to the left of the trainer, who meanwhile slowly proceeds in the direction A–E. We must ensure that this zigzag method is practised from the start. The dog, as soon as he has cornered the 'criminal' on the right, must not then be over-excited by him, otherwise, when the trainer returns with the animal to the main direction to continue quartering, the dog will be too strongly attracted towards the right, whereas the second course must go left. Accordingly, the dog is only allowed to bay the 'criminal' for a short time and is then put down near him, whereupon the animal's experience tells it that no further exciting events are to be expected. The 'criminal' now moves slowly away and the trainer begins to walk back to the starting point with the dog. To ensure that the animal will, when quartering is resumed, run to the left, the 'criminal' who has been under cover may emerge from his hiding-place and take a few steps forward. As soon as the dog, if necessary attracted by a noise, notices him, he should immediately run back into hiding, the trainer meanwhile once more giving the necessary signals and running a few steps with the dog in that direction. Cornering, baying and the down follow as in the case of the 'criminal' on the right. Trainer and dog then return to the central direction. The 'criminal' on the right has meanwhile, without entering the area to be quartered, taken up a position at the end of the next right-hand point and the dog is again sent off in the lateral direction right. Frequent changes of the persons acting as criminals are essential.

As soon as the dog shows a tendency to take the right and left courses alternately of its own accord, the 'criminals' no longer emerge and make no further noise. Training under these conditions being satisfactory, blind courses, that is, those with no 'criminal' at the ends of them, are introduced. As training advances, more and more attention is paid to the exercises which follow the actions of cornering and baying, so that the dog may become familiar with all the events that follow picking up hidden criminals.

(c) *Object reconnaissance.*

If the intention is to train the dog in such a way that with certain signals he will search for objects only, procedure will be based, as already mentioned, on a properly mastered retrieve and will be developed by the use of appropriate signals, just as in the case of human reconnaissance.

2. TRACKING

(a) *Services available.*

In a state of nature the dog hunts in various ways. Sometimes he finds prey through the body-scent directly emitted from it. If he strikes this scent by chance, he makes his way towards it with raised muzzle. He may also find his prey through the track-scent it leaves behind and this he follows with muzzle to the ground. At a certain distance from the prey body-scent may again come into action, but ear and eye now also play a part. Memory, too, helps: places are looked for that the animal's experience tells him are frequented by prey. Searching and finding in this way we can simply call hunting.

As it is advantageous for many human purposes to restrict finding methods to a single type, the dog is trained accordingly. Such is the origin of simple tracking work. The dog in this case finds only with his nose, using exclusively the track-scent left by a living creature that is moving forward some distance ahead. Work with the nose can, however, be restricted still further by giving the dog training in persisting on a certain track in pursuit of a single scent peculiar to that particular track.

A human being moving forward in open country emits a number of different scents. In walking, footprints are usually left on the ground. If so, layers of earth are uncovered which are usually damper than the undisturbed surface of the soil. For this reason there is considerable evaporation where the foot falls and the smell of earth is consequently stronger. The character of this earth-smell may also be different from that at the undisturbed spots, owing to the uncovering of decomposing organic matter under the surface of the soil. The strength of such a track-scent is in itself variable: the pressure of footprints may be different—a man may be walking or running, light or heavy on his feet, and the surface of the soil may vary in impressionability. The strength and character of track-scents may also vary because of the difference in the types of ground traversed. Such changes in strength and character of a track-scent may occur in the course of the same track.

If undergrowth is present, plants are trodden down in walking. The considerable degree of moisture given off by the damaged plants results in a stronger plant-smell than at places where no such damage has been done. In this case, too, the strength and character of the plant-smell and of the track-scent may vary in accordance with the quantity and type of undergrowth present. These changes may also occur in the course of a single track. Further, a booted foot always smells of leather, and particles of the material used in tanning, as well as of shoe polish, adhere to the ground, as the boots press and rub against the surface of the soil and the undergrowth. These scents, too, may change in strength and character according to the type of footwear and the way in which it has been treated. Changes of this kind do not normally occur in the course of a single track. There are no such scents, of course, in the case of a bare-footed walker.

The track-scent may also involve subsidiary smells, due to contact of the boots with something that gives off odour, for instance dung and insects. Changes in the course of a single track are again possible in this case.

The track of a human being is therefore composed of various

scents which may undergo considerable and abrupt changes. Stony or frozen earth covered with snow may also be encountered, as well as ice with or without snow. Moreover, variations in track-scent may arise as a result of differences in age and weather.

All such changes can be successfully dealt with by the animal's nose after sufficient practice.

There are, however, other scents on a human track which always remain the same throughout: the specifically human smell that comes through the boots and includes the personal or individual scent. We are aware today that under certain circumstances a dog may be able to recognize individual scents while tracking and distinguish one from another. This faculty should enable us to keep a dog to a single track.

When an animal has a certain kind of experience, for instance when it notices changes in scent, its reaction *may* be visible to us. But if no such reaction is, in fact, visible, we cannot be certain that no change of scent has been noticed. It would be an error always to suppose that consciousness of scent changes is at once followed by visible reaction.

Still further from the truth is the view which assumes that all such reactions must be of a character useful to a human being. This attitude is responsible for the belief in imaginary 'crime dogs' which, when set to follow an unknown track, stick to it without changing over to any other human tracks. We realize today, especially while on service, that the apparent ability of these dogs is due to the trainer's previous knowledge of the task in view, and is misinterpreted because of ignorance of the actual sense-stimuli that operate on the animal.

If dogs change over from one human track to another, it is not necessarily because they have failed to recognize variations in scent. Before assuming this to be the case we must ask whether these animals have been *trained* to give a visible reaction whenever there is a change of scent. A dog has now to be trained, as it never was formerly, for the express purpose of keeping to a single track. Even on a familiar track, for example that of its own master, the dog does not necessarily follow the personal or individual scent of the man he knows. The animal must first be specially taught to develop this capacity, which we will call *track-fidelity*. He may learn it either by training or by his own experience. Track-fidelity on the track of the trainer, as a consequence of training, can be relied on if the track of the trainer and those which lead away from it are all of the same age; but no such reliance can be placed on track-fidelity based on the dog's own experience. As a rule the animal does not have the chance of contracting the habit of following the personal scent in a track to the exclusion of all others. There are plenty of other ways in which the trainer can be located, but these are rarely taken into consideration when explaining how the dog has found. The mistaken opinion that the dog must necessarily follow the track of its trainer because of the *personal* scent, arose from a comparison of the commonly observed ease with which the dog recognizes its own trainer by his individual body-scent. This body-scent, however, is neither in strength nor other qualities identical with the personal scent which is conveyed through the boots and mingled with other track-scents.

Track-fidelity to a stranger's track is still more difficult to develop. It has been noted in some few animals, but fidelity to the track of either trainer or stranger has only been achieved in favourable conditions, which are hardly ever to be found on active service.

Track-fidelity should not be used as a foundation for developing tracking ability on active service.

Dogs which do not persist on the initial track and do not reject other human tracks may be called track-happy. They change over from the initial track to others as fresh or fresher. These animals do not feel bound to follow any particular scent-component of the track. On the contrary, any of the usual scent-components of a human track will, as a rule, suffice to initiate pursuit. This will even occur when there is no characteristic or personal human scent. Even then track-happy dogs usually pursue without hesitation the track-scents which are available, for instance those of damaged plants and footprints.

Track-happy dogs are by no means to be considered inferior. They not only do a useful job in tracking the perpetrators of recent crimes, but also facilitate the choice of animals suitable for tracking, improving the breed by natural selection. Finally, they give pleasure to anyone who is in any way interested in tracking.

Persistence upon the initial track is certainly important, particularly in detective work. It is possible to train dogs in such a way that they will, with a high degree of reliability, persist upon old human tracks several miles long where there are few other tracks of the same age. A time interval as short as three minutes between the initial track and the rest may secure persistence, while with a ten-minutes' difference persistence on the initial track is, as a rule, assured.

Dogs trained not to switch between older and later tracks may be called *track-sure*. It is not yet quite certain which scent is decisive for the track-sure dog. No doubt the variations of scent caused, by the time differences have something to do with it. The track-sure dog is exclusively concerned with human tracks and takes note of objects lying on the track only if they bear human scent. It does not necessarily follow, however, in such cases, that the object indicated has been in contact with the person providing the track.

Canine nose work has been considerably improved of late years owing to the light which new knowledge has thrown on this field. We may for instance refer to the results obtained in the indication of scent conformity or similarity. We should also mention the new conclusions reached regarding the composition of tracks and their possible effects on training. Today we may speak of setting the dog upon a certain scent-component of the human track. Track-fidelity is also considered here. Finally, we may refer to the exercises which attempt to achieve persistence on the initial track without the aid of any specific and personal human scent. The result of these attempts has been the track-sure dog. With the help of such an animal, as already stated, it is possible to follow for distances of several miles human tracks crossed by a large number of other tracks and dating back much further than was previously considered possible.

In working experiments with track-sure dogs the following results were obtained. No tracking could be undertaken on a dry stone surface or on asphalt. If such surfaces are wet the dog can only track for quite short distances. The same applies to dry sandy ground with or without undergrowth. Damp sand, even without undergrowth, will, on the contrary, hold a track in favourable weather for as long as twelve hours. On ground

L

overgrown with grass and vegetation a track will hold in favourable weather, that is in moist air and moderate winds, but with no sunshine, as long as twenty-four hours. On the other hand, dry air, a high wind and hot sunshine in regions without shade will sometimes obliterate a track after so brief a period as three hours. In the same weather conditions, with shady trees and protection from the wind, tracks as old as twelve hours can be followed up. In open country, unprotected from the wind but otherwise favourable, a high wind may obliterate tracks in three hours. In the same conditions, but with trees and wind protection, tracks will hold about seven hours. Tracks laid after sunset will frequently remain in good shape until the next morning, before the ground dries. These are called overnight tracks. In frost, tracks on snow last longer than tracks where the snow has melted. If snow falls on tracks they may sometimes hold till the fresh snow is about an inch and a half deep. Depths exceeding this level mean that the track-scent has been obliterated. Downpours and rains of long duration extinguish track-scent, while light showers facilitate tracking. A heavy frost has no unfavourable influence on such work.

Police tracking dogs have rendered outstanding services in detection but their abilities may be said to be capable of further development by additional research on tracking and by scientific breeding. Tough dogs of good constitution, which take intense pleasure in retrieving and tracking and show first-rate judgment in distinguishing between scents, are needed for this work. To ensure good performance the appropriate building of the character of the dog while it is performing other duties is essential. In this work the proper training in service requirements of the handlers plays an important part.

(b) *General.*

Methods of training for tracking are dictated by the object in view. In all this work the dog must learn to use only his nose and not his eye or ear.

In the fourth edition of my *Introduction to Dog Training* published in Germany in 1917 I wrote:

'In tracking, the service which the dog should perform is the provision, after a crime, of clues to identify the culprit.

Neither pursuit nor seizure nor any baying of the male-factor is feasible. All that is possible at present is the fol-lowing up of the track or parts of it. The game of looking for lost objects could be used for this purpose. This exercise does not stimulate the predatory instincts of the dog and is, therefore, undertaken by the animal with less impetu-osity and more careful use of its sense of smell. If, in such a case, the dog were set to work by signals (sounds and gestures) associated with looking for lost objects, he would naturally also pick up anything lying within the scent-range of the track, which would be by no means a disadvantage.'

In the same edition the topic of tracking for objects is treated thus:

'Looking for lost objects is of value because it perfects the dog's tracking work. In looking for persons, finding conditions are easier. The dog will succeed in finding by merely keeping cursorily to the course of the track, for the scent given out by a human being is so strong that the animal cannot fail to notice it. Scenting conditions are con-siderably modified, however, when objects giving out a good deal less scent lie on the track. To find these articles the sense of smell has to be more powerfully exerted. There is another circumstance which will improve reliability in keeping to the track when objects are being sought for. The exciting anticipation of meeting an enemy is lacking and conse-quently the search for objects is carried out at a gradually decreasing rate of movement.'

These principles are still valid today for work in tracking human beings. At that time the training of the guard dog was not separated from that of the tracking dog. Since then this separation has followed on efforts to improve canine capa-bilities. (Separation of the training of the guard dog from that of the tracking dog was instigated by Böttger in 1915.)

The tracking instinct of the dog is affected by other canine instincts. For example, tracking may be instigated by the in-stinct for prey. In tracking human beings hostility to the persons concerned as well as the track-scent would be the original inducement, as would inanimate objects regarded as prey, the seizing and fetching of which are familiar to the animal through his previous training. The best work in tracking human beings is achieved by means of the finding of objects and with application of compulsion.

The tracking instinct can also be aroused through the pack instinct, if either the trainer or an acquaintance belonging to the dog's pack-circle acts as a primary inducement by moving away from the animal and then letting it find him. But this type of training is, like the finding of hostile persons, only feasible when the dog is on the lead. Otherwise it will dash off at full speed and there will be no chance beforehand of applying inducement to use the nose only on the track.

In this connection the difference between body-scent and track-scent when using the nose should be noticed. The difference is worth illustrating. Fig. 18 indicates the influence of body-scent on the use of the nose upwind. The dog should be set to the track at A. At this point the animal can only make use of the track-scent left on the ground. It must, therefore, put its nose down in order to track. But this will not be necessary when the dog gets as far as L. For there the contrary wind has driven the body-scent down the track. With a high wind this may be the case over long distances. It would be absurd for the trainer to attempt to force the dog to keep its nose to the ground, since, from the animal's point of view, it has already located its quarry by body-scent. It will follow the scent with lifted muzzle and find in the same way. This will happen even if the concealed person is sitting or lying down, and can be obviated only by the use of very small and very slightly odorous objects.

The position is quite different when the track is laid downwind. As shown in Fig. 19, body-scent is now blown up the track, so that the animal does not become aware of it till he is directly in front of the concealed person or object.

Understanding of the influence of body-scent on the dog is important. On the one hand it will prevent the trainer mistakenly requiring the dog to hold its nose down to pick up track-scent when body-scent is available, and on the other will show him the necessity of laying the track, *or the end* of the track, downwind, for otherwise he will not be able to achieve

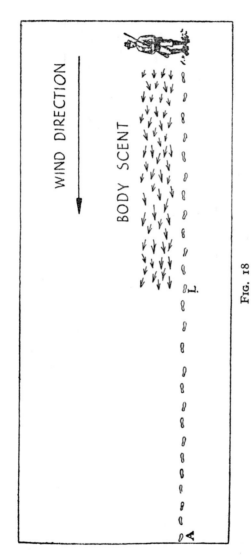

Fig. 18

Tracking upwind

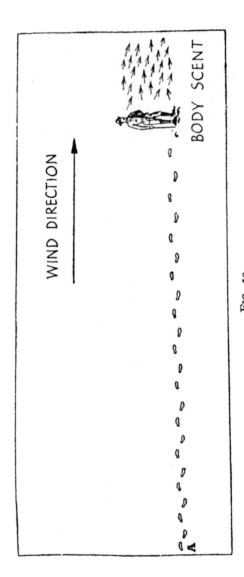

FIG. 19

Tracking downwind

use of the nose for track-scent alone. Since the wind at ground level often shifts, great care should always be taken, especially at the beginning of training, to check the direction of the wind.

A dog that is often given opportunities of finding by body-scent in wind will contract the habit of raising his muzzle to sniff the wind. Other undesirable consequences are that eye and ear are too readily resorted to in the work.

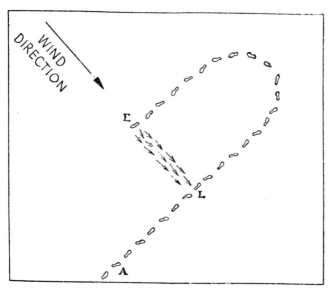

FIG. 20

A curving track

If in the course of training tracks are laid in curves or with corners, due attention should always be paid to the influence of body-scent. If, for example, a curving track has to be followed, a dog set on at A (*see* Fig. 20) will, unless the distance from L to E is too great, already be in receipt, at L, of the body-scent of the persons or object at E. The animal has therefore found on arrival at L. It will, accordingly, thenceforth make directly for E without following up the curve of the track and should, of course, be permitted to do so.

Even if the curve of the track had been laid downwind, the dog would still have found by body-scent, as shown in

Fig. 21. For if a wind at ground level is blowing laterally across the track and the track is fresh, the dog will follow not along the track but to one side of it. Consequently he will not find at E but at h, where he gets the body-scent. He would, however, have found by track-scent if the end of the track had been prolonged from E to cross h. The pursuit of wind-blown tracks

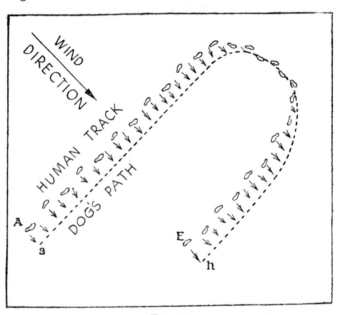

FIG. 21

Wind blowing across track

to one side instead of along their courses is, perhaps, accounted for as follows. The dog does not keep his nose at the centre of the track-scent area but at its edge, because there the scent can always be picked up afresh by snuffing up 'non-stimulant' air. The dog does not, therefore, keep his nose down when working on powerfully odorous or fresh tracks, but does do so when the tracks are weak or old.

So-called overshooting, of fresh tracks in particular, need not be regarded as a fault. Fig. 22 illustrates this point. The dog is working up the track from A and overshoots it at B, as the wind is driving the scent some distance beyond B. At C

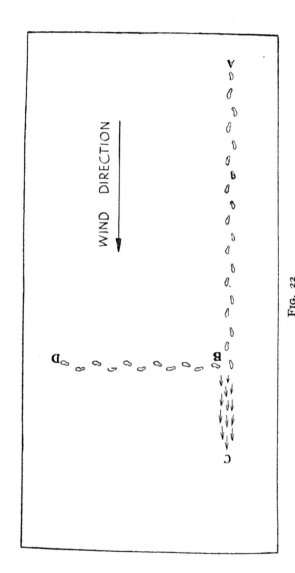

FIG. 22

Overshooting a fresh track

the scent is lost. The dog then doubles. In doing so it may very easily happen that he does not take the direction towards D but follows a lateral one which is not that of the track, with the result that the track must then be sought and found afresh before work can proceed. Overshooting is also possible in the case of *old* tracks which are being worked by dogs at speed, without leads.

Irregularities in terrain often influence wind direction. The direction of the wind on slopes, in valleys and hollows and behind woods is often entirely different from that which prevails at higher levels. These circumstances influence nose work and sometimes cause the dog apparently to deviate from the track-scent when the track is strongly odorous. It may be noted that if there is no wind, body-scent will hang in the air for a brief period, especially over ground protected from air currents. It lasts, however, for a few minutes at most. Body-scent is then dispersed and loses its effect on the dog. Body-scent which may drop from body to ground is also ineffective in the production of track-scent. But the parts of the body above the feet have to be considered among those retaining body-scent when they come in contact with features of the terrain, for instance vegetation when high enough. This type of ground should be avoided while teaching tracking.

The trainer will soon get into the way of looking to see whether the dog has its nose to the track-scent or not. He will also soon be able to judge whether the dog is holding its nose high to assist seeing or hearing, or whether this attitude is a sign that the animal has picked up body-scent.

To ensure that the nose alone is used in tracking, a few further points should be borne in mind.

Finding by aid of eye or ear should not be allowed. Consequently, the object to be found must always be rendered quite invisible. If track-layers are being used they should take care not to reveal themselves by either movement or noise.

To prevent the dog finding by memory, training should take place in extensive open country or, if only smallish areas are available, the site should be frequently changed. To avoid the association of external stimuli with the exercise, the dog should only rarely be permitted to find where there is some conspicuous object in the landscape, for example a house, a solitary bush or a tree.

Distractions should at first be avoided, so far as practicable, unless under the direction of an expert trainer. Dogs learn to track while on the lead. If left to itself the animal would often take to hunting and might then easily find by body-scent or by eye, which would render it less amenable to the habit of using the nose alone in tracking. Until this habit has become second nature, the following should be borne in mind. Training should take place on terrain where ground conditions (woods, meadows, fields, patches of grass) are extremely favourable. The trainer must then *know* the course of the track *down to the last detail*, otherwise he will be unable to apply the proper inducements to the animal. Certain points on the terrain should be chosen for marking the path taken by the track-layer. His starting-place should be precisely known. Care must be taken, however, in any such marking, to prevent the production of visual or olfactory stimuli not found on active service. The earth, for instance, should not be scraped up.

A start is made with short tracks of about thirty paces, which are at first laid in a straight line. Zigzag tracks should not be laid if tracks are no more than an hour old, otherwise they will create a whole field of scent, which will impede the dog's attempts to follow up the track. He would be more or less likely, depending on the air currents, to cut the corners.

In the case of track-happy dogs one must *continually* remember that persistence on the initial track can only be relied on when the other tracks within scenting range are considerably weaker in their odours. Careful attention should be paid to this point during training. During training a dog should only rarely be allowed to follow up a track without finding anything, otherwise his interest in tracking will diminish. Cases when nothing is found may well be left for active service; the exercises in which the animal finds regularly will prevent the association established from disintegrating. The objects to be found during tracking must always be carefully laid on the track itself, not to right or left of it, for should the dog find, by body-scent, objects off the track, the requisite concentration on track-scent would be prejudiced. Objects should not be laid where the track takes a turn, otherwise two disadvantages will ensue. In the first place, an undesirable association might easily be formed between the finding of an object and the turn of the track, while in the second place a dog may often fail to scent an object lying at the turn, particularly when the direction of the wind, if the track is fresh, causes the corner to be cut. In the case of a fresh track this may also occur when the object lies just in front of, or just behind, the bend. A dog often fails to find an object just behind the bend when the track is strongly odorous, because he overshoots (*see* Fig. 22) the track. He then has to cast about before he can take it up again. In this process he will often end up on the regained track several paces distant from the corner.

The objects should be as inconspicuous as possible and not easily distinguishable in colour or shape from the ground.

The purpose of training is to teach the dog to notice and pick up only objects bearing human scent. To prevent the dog reacting to canine as well as to human scent we should not use any objects which the dog has brought in before.

The following Sections include the necessary information on the use of the trainer's own track for making the dog familiar with this work:

(c) *Training the track-happy dog.*

Training must proceed on the lead until the dog has been fully trained to the work, otherwise it will be impossible to apply the compulsive inducements indispensable for ensuring first-rate performance. If we achieve our purpose we shall be able, very occasionally and in special cases, to work with a lead dragging on the ground or, in the case of dogs that move slowly on the track, in the absence of inducements from the trainer, who can follow on foot without exertion, with none at all.

A large number of the dogs trained for tracking have previously been used to working with eye and ear as well, and to finding by body-scent. Such animals have to be induced to use the nose exclusively. The dog must not be allowed to relapse into his former method of hunting but must be made to keep his nose down, without dashing ahead, and may have to be given special training before he will go forward at all.

For this purpose the equipment recommended by Böttger

is admirably suited. A thirty-foot lead is hooked into a ring immediately behind the chest harness and carried between the dog's hind-legs. This arrangement best enables the requisite jerking inducements to the lead to be applied. A jerk on the lead brings the animal's head down if it is using its eyes or ears and prevents it from relapsing into hunting. If the dog dashes forward at speed the chain-collar automatically causes pain, since the trainer always follows at a normal foot-pace in order that the animal may gradually learn to work slowly. Finally, an upward jerk of the lead induces the dog to go forward if it has come to a halt.

Distractions are avoided so far as possible until the dog has reached the stage of training at which the exclusive use of the nose for tracking can be brought about by compulsion. The dog must never be allowed to watch or listen to the tracks being laid, or to observe the placing of the objects, by the track-layer.

The best plan is for the trainer himself to lay the first tracks. The setting of the dog on the personal human scent (individual scent) included in the track is arranged as follows. The animal can only be so set if it is trained in such a way that it does not switch from the trainer's track to strangers' tracks of the same age, otherwise it will never develop track-fidelity. Moreover, unless the animal is given practice in not switching to older or newer tracks, it cannot be set on the scent of a track of any given age. The dog will, therefore, never be track-sure.

A track-happy dog is guided by the most outstanding odours of the track, as a rule those of downtrodden vegetation and footprinted earth, and not by those of human type and still less by individual human odour. Nevertheless, the track laid by the trainer has the following advantages. The trainer needs no assistants. He has the best possible practice in tracing the course of the track. He is bound to give the course of the track careful consideration, if only because it is his own dog that he is teaching.

We must not assume that the use of strangers' tracks, which is taken up as training proceeds, confronts the dog with a new lesson. It will take to and follow up the track, from the first, exactly as if it were the trainer's. For the animal, after all, has not been by any means concentrating on a *personal* scent.

Among the distractions which should be avoided, in addition to those of visual and auditory type, are those of an olfactory nature, for instance tracks of game. To begin with, country as far as possible free from tracks should be found. In the case of the track-happy dog, constant care must be taken that the scent of the initial track does not include that of any fresher tracks or any of the same age, but only such track-scents as are at least half an hour older than the initial track.

Training is begun with fresh, and consequently strong-scented, tracks from five to ten minutes old. In order to arouse a powerful tracking instinct in the dog the layer of the track should walk to and fro, without shuffling, in a circle of about half a square yard and then, immediately afterwards, begin to lay the track. Shuffling has to be avoided to prevent the production of excessive odours such as those of damaged plants and pressed-down earth. The track-layer then goes about fifteen paces in a straight line, lays an object on the track, then goes ahead again for about another fifteen paces. He then turns back, making a detour, to ensure that the return track lies sufficiently far from the initial track as not to point in the same direction. Distances should, of course, differ as required with lateral, head or following wind.

Tracks are at first laid upwind. This arrangement causes the track-scent to reach the dog, thereby arousing its tracking instinct, as soon as the animal nears the track and also facilitates following up. Another advantage is that the dog very rapidly picks up the scent of the object coming downwind to him. Initially, this experience should ensue soon after the start of tracking, so as to arouse the tracking instinct by means of the disposition to retrieve. As training proceeds what was said on the subject of wind direction should be borne in mind. Olfactory awareness of the object may at first be facilitated for the dog by the use of articles that have a fairly strong scent. Leather, for instance, emits a powerful scent. Apart from this point, objects should be chosen to begin with which the dog enjoys picking up.

As soon as the track has become from five to ten minutes old, the trainer takes his stand with the dog, held at first on a short lead, behind the place where the track starts. When the animal begins to sniff, a loud, caressing 'Seek' is uttered, accompanied by the particular gestures appropriate to tracking. At the same moment the lead is allowed to run out. When united with the auditory signal 'Seek' the gestures will, in the course of training, come to form secondary inducements and signals for the start of tracking.

If the animal takes to the track at the inducements given, the trainer follows, holding the lead loosely. If the dog neither sniffs at the starting-point nor takes to the track, the trainer walks, holding the animal quite short on the lead, along the track, repeating the word 'Seek' in a friendly tone and making the necessary gestures. In many cases the dog, by reason of its previous habits, may at first show little inclination to track but keep its head high, so as to use eye and ear. If the animal shows the slightest sign of using its nose, the sound of encouragement should be uttered, together with a friendly 'Seek', but replaced by a harsh tone if the dog lifts its muzzle, while looking and listening as though scenting the wind, provided this behaviour is not associated with becoming aware of any object laid on the track. The noticing and picking up of the object is always to be made agreeable by prolonged fondling.

In this training the stage reached by the dog in retrieving must be taken into consideration. We may, for example, to save time, begin tracking even with a dog that is still not quite reliable in the retrieving of small and uncongenial objects. In this case we shall have to dispense with meticulously accurate picking up and surrendering of the object. Were any kind of compulsion to be used in connection with picking up or retrieving during tracking work, the tracking instinct would be impaired. A dog, therefore, which is not yet reliable in retrieving must be treated as follows.

When the dog approaches the object, his behaviour on picking up its scent is observed. If he picks up the object of his own accord, the phrase 'There's a good boy' is uttered and further enthusiastic expressions of satisfaction are used. If the dog then drops the object, nothing should be done to cause him to pick it up again, but inducements should continue to proceed with tracking. If the dog retains the object in his jaws, he is gently instigated to give it up and then at once induced to proceed with tracking. The animal should never be allowed to associate the finding of an object with the cessation of tracking.

For this reason tracking should never be concluded on the finding of an object. It should always be taken a stage further.

If the dog does not pick up the object, the auxiliary sound 'Fetch it' should instantly be uttered. This sound must only be made at the instant when it is desired that the dog should seize the object; never at the start of tracking or at any other time during tracking. The auxiliary sound is dropped altogether as soon as the dog picks up of its own accord. If 'Fetch it' has no effect, an inducement used in retrieving exercises should be revived. The object is immediately kicked, so that it moves and becomes active to some extent. It may also be thrown a little way up the track. If this action, too, proves of no effect, no further inducement should be made to pick up. The training should be stopped and exercises be renewed later with a fresh straight track and the object laid in the same way. The activation of the object is regularly resorted to, in rapid succession if necessary, if the dog does not pick up either of its own accord or on the words 'Fetch it'. If after two or three days our efforts are still unsuccessful, the dog is not yet sufficiently reliable on retrieving and the training will either have to be abandoned or we must be satisfied with the mere persistence of the dog on the track. In any case, the retrieve will have to be brought up to the necessary standard at a time and place unassociated with tracking.

If the dog's progress has been sufficient to enable it to pick up different kinds of small objects, tracks may be prolonged in proportion to the progress made. They can also be laid with curves and corners. The same track must never be used twice running, or the dog will become accustomed to set tracks and memory will then play a part in its work. Regular, methodical changes of tracking plans are essential.

When tracks are prolonged, the lead may be let further and further out. Several objects, too, may be laid. They should always be arranged at irregular distances from one another but never less than fifty yards apart. Objects should be progressively restricted to those having a weak scent.

Something remains to be said about the over-running of objects. If there is a current of wind at the spot on the track where the object lies the dog often fails to find it. This may occur, for instance, when the object lies close to the bole of a tree. Finding is often also impossible because the dog, naturally, does not scent when it is breathing out. Capricious winds or changing currents of air produced by a ground wind are also frequent causes of the dog over-running.

If the dog overshoots the object, counter-inducements can only be applied if the trainer is quite certain that the animal has noticed the object but has not picked it up. In that case the measures previously described are undertaken. If, on the other hand, the object has been over-run for normal reasons, the track should be quietly followed up to the end, for the continuity of tracking should never be interrupted if it can be avoided. Another reason is that if the dog has, in fact, failed to scent the object, that is, not noticed it at all, any kind of compulsion to pick up would prejudice the dog's enjoyment of tracking. This disadvantage can only be accepted if the dog does not pick up the object although he has noticed it. Particular attention should be paid to the fact that, as indicated earlier, the dog does not invariably work exactly *on* a fresh track; for example when there is a lateral wind or he overshoots a corner. This behaviour must be distinguished from cases when the dog, as for instance after overshooting a corner, does not resume the lost track, but takes to hunting. In the last case a sternly uttered 'Seek' or stronger compulsion by tugging at the lead should be instantly employed, followed at once by 'There's a good boy' if the dog makes an effort to pick up the track again. This sound of encouragement is once more repeated, in rapid succession, if he resumes the track.

Compulsion, in a stronger or weaker form, will be found essential with many dogs if good service in tracking is to be obtained from them. It is not only a question of achieving the exclusive use of the nose. The inclination to track can itself be increased by properly applied compulsion, once the dog has arrived at a stage when he is aware that he can at once escape compulsion by the use of the nose. As training proceeds, compulsion must also be applied whenever the dog yields to other inclinations, if he sniffs at a mousehole, for instance. If a dog is fairly capable a flick with the switch and a 'Bah!', followed by 'There's a good boy' as the tracking is resumed, is perfectly legitimate.

As soon as tracking is carried out reliably the type of objects

M

used should be changed, as should the distances between them. Objects which are conspicuous on the ground owing to their colour should only rarely be used. The finding of buried objects presents no difficulty; on the contrary, if the objects have been buried by hand or foot, it is simple, for the human scent is then far stronger at the spots where they are concealed than elsewhere. Even if objects are buried with a spade, the hiding-place is closely surrounded by footprints, so that if a dog has occasionally to dig up objects hidden on a track the experience, though new, is not one of special difficulty. But such exercises should be practised only occasionally.

The age up to which tracks are worked will depend upon the service required. Tracks up to two hours old are considered fresh.

(*d*) *Free tracking by the track-happy dog.*

Provided the general purpose of training is not prejudiced, where it is desired to let a dog track while off the lead, a single object only should be laid on any one track which is to be worked out, for the finding of this object always ends the track—the dog returning forthwith to the trainer with the object it has picked up. It is recommended that work should begin on the lead, to facilitate inducement to perform as required. An intermediate stage may consist in allowing the lead to drag along the ground. With this procedure the dog continues to feel dependent upon the trainer and will behave in a more orderly fashion than it would if working in complete freedom. A preliminary condition for work at liberty is that the dog should already be reliable in retrieving the kind of objects placed on the tracks. To begin with, the object used is similar in colour to that of the ground but possesses a strong scent, otherwise the dog, which at first often tracks in a very slap-dash manner, will be very liable to over-run the object. A small piece of wood, for example, covered with earth-coloured leather, would be suitable. We must put up with the disadvantage that the dog will at first be concentrating upon one particular object and, in addition, upon his own canine scent, which is, of course, borne by the repeatedly used object. This method is unsuitable in teaching a dog to be track-sure.

The training begins, as described in Section (*c*), with short, straight tracks and proceeds until retrieving of the object can be relied on. Tracks should not be laid in the neighbourhood of distinctive environmental stimuli.

If, when free tracking commences, the dog tends to relapse into hunting, the objects are arranged in such a way, so far as may be possible, to prevent his finding by this means. For example, the track may be laid straight to begin with then be made to turn right at a right angle and finally, after a suitable distance, to end with another right-angled turn to the right. The object should be laid on this last lap, so that it is to be found in the opposite direction to that of the first lap of the track. The dog should always be called off immediately it starts hunting.

Should it be the intention to use the dog for tracking male-factors, no track-layer should ever be allowed to remain any-where about the territory when objects are being tracked free. He should turn back to where the trainer is standing. This is necessary because were the dog to catch up with the track-layer, as he might when over-running an object, the animal might easily be reminded of past experiences which occurred after persons were found during tracking. The consequence would be the baying of the cornered man.

Since in free tracking it frequently happens that the dog at first over-runs an object owing to impetuosity and inade-quate use of the nose, we must beware of treating the animal, when he comes up to the trainer, with any degree of severity. Quite apart from the fact that over-running is easily possible for reasons given in Section (c), any show of severity in such circum-stances would be likely to produce an undesirable association with the recall. The dog must, therefore, always be received with caresses and 'There's a good boy', though he may have over-run the object and completed the rest of the track. If one is uncertain why the object was not picked up, one should allow the dog to work the track to the end, for in the case of an over-run object a disagreeable experience, e.g. a 'Bah!' or a call-off, would be prejudicial to the working out of the track itself. On any occasion when the dog fails to pick up an object, whether he over-runs it or leaves it owing to insufficient training in the retrieve, it is always advisable to put the dog on the lead for the second working out of the track. If a second working out

M*

takes place without the lead, the animal may be expected to make imperfect use of its sense of smell for, of course, it already knows the way, and may even at the second working out of the track fail to find the object. But if the lead is used the trainer can, by resorting to the sounds of correction and encouragement, induce the animal to work much more effectively.

If the dog leaves the track again we must ascertain whether such action is due to any dispersion of the scent, owing to a side wind, for instance, or to the animal ceasing to follow the track-scent and relapsing into hunting. The question can be decided according to whether or not the dog, on leaving the track after over-running a corner, immediately begins to search for the scent again, keeping his head low. If he starts hunting, a harsh 'Seek', several times repeated, is uttered, followed by a 'There's a good boy' as soon as the dog makes an effort to pick up the line again. The sound of encouragement is again repeated as soon as he reaches the track and begins to follow it up once more. If the harsh 'Seek' has no effect, the dog must be called off, agreeable experience only being provided on this occasion, and after an interval tracking with the lead should be resumed.

(e) *Training the track-sure dog.*

If we wish to achieve the highest degree of perfection in tracking we must renounce versatility. The police dog on track duty should only employ the nose. His instinct to guard is completely in abeyance. During training he should never experience hostility from those who accompany him on the track.

The purpose of training is that the dog should use its nose as continuously as possible and with complete concentration on the scent belonging to the initial track. To do this he must scent the track step by step, for which object Böttger's track-harness is the best method of teaching (*see* Fig. 23). The course of the track should be arranged to include plenty of angles and corners. Further, the exclusive use of very small and quite lightly scented objects, differing as little as possible from the ground in colour and shape, is desirable. Again, after training has reached a certain stage, practice should take place on tracks which are not less than two hours old and which oblige the dog to make the most painstaking use of his nose. In this connection, too, care should be taken to practise on ground which varies both in type and vegetation. The dog should be given plenty of opportunity to pick up the scent at the start of the course. Persistence on an initial track being a prime object of training, it is particularly important always to have a precise and detailed knowledge of the course, to avoid unsuitable inducements. The finishing touch to training comes when the trainer knows neither the start of the track nor anything at all about its course. When that stage is reached trainer and dog have been welded into a perfect unity and are capable of performing the best type of service.

FIG. 23
Böttger's track-harness

On active service the method of setting the dog on the track will depend on the ability it shows, an essential preliminary condition being the availability of scent from human footprints. The track is provided by a series of advancing footsteps, whether each individual imprint is visible or not. We always speak of tracks and not of traces, since the latter expression covers *all* indications left behind by the malefactor or created by him.

Before the dog is set on the track, the scene of the crime must be searched to discover what kind of ground the perpetrator has stepped on, such as earth, grass, wood or stone. If the dog has to be set on invisible tracks its persistence on the initial track cannot, of course, be checked with certainty. Consequently, it is of special importance in such cases to discover whether other persons have visited the scene and covered the malefactor's scent with their own.

Appropriate districts for practice are flat and easily surveyed, with a few landmarks, such as single trees or bushes, to show the course of the track. Dry, flat, sandy places, without undergrowth, and stone or asphalt pavements or the like, are unsuitable.

The experienced trainer, or pupils attending a course of training, may undertake even initial training under the following distractions.

Strangers may be allowed to wander about the district selected for training. Fairly loud noises, such as those of heavy lorries, may be heard. Tracks and droppings of game, as well as strange dogs, may also be present.

The inexperienced trainer, working to a book, should delay training with distractions until the dog has worked out shortish tracks and can be relied on to retrieve objects of its own accord. Such a trainer should not at first include distracting tracks in his work and should abide by the principles laid down in Sections (b) and (c).

The dog can also be trained in such a way that instead of picking up objects found in the scent-area of the track he will merely indicate them by standing still or sitting down.

The first tracks are laid as recommended in Section (c). As soon as the dog will start on a track of its own accord a straight track should be laid downwind or in an area protected from the wind, so that the body-scent of objects is not carried to the dog and its nose, especially on fresh tracks, must be kept close to the ground. One must be particularly careful in the choice of objects, which should invariably be quite small and inconspicuous. In order that they may carry human scent, they should always be kept on one's own person, in the trouser pocket. They should never be used more than once and should be put away in a place where the dog will not be able to notice them again in future training. If used more than once they naturally come to bear canine scent after being held in the dog's jaws. Pieces of bark an inch or two long and about half an inch thick, such as may be found lying about in woods, are very suitable for the purpose. Fallen twigs of about this size are equally suitable. Their ends, however, should not be cut off, in case some colour contrasting with that of the ground should then be exposed. Buttons with a dull surface and of inconspicuous colouring are also quite useful.

We begin with fresh tracks ten or fifteen minutes old, which may be those laid by the trainer or handler. Concentration on individual scent does not accompany the type of training given. Work on the trainer's track may continue until we reach the stage at which the dog is so far advanced that thenceforth the courses of the tracks are unknown to the trainer.

As soon as sufficient progress has been made in the use of the nose for tracking to be attained by compulsive inducement, the inexperienced trainer working alone may deal with cross-tracks, at first only with those not more than half an hour older than the initial track. This chronological difference is gradually decreased to a few minutes. Not till later should cross-tracks that are fresher than the main track be introduced. The dog should then still be only working tracks more than two hours old. Once he reaches tracks of that age he should never again be put to work on fresher ones. We may again emphasize that in dealing with this stage of training it is most important to have a precise knowledge of the course of the initial track. Otherwise one might not apply the correct inducements when the dog at first shows an inclination to pick up cross-tracks. The degree of compulsion required will depend upon the temperament and capacity of the dog in question. The weaker form consists of a harsh 'Seek', while the stronger is accompanied by a jerk at the lead. Strong compulsion should not be used to induce persistence. Compulsion must always be followed by agreeable experience immediately the dog behaves as desired.

In training for persistence on the track the dog should be made to concentrate on the scent relating to the initial track; this probably being of a different age from the rest. Consequently, cross-tracks of the same age should be avoided as far as possible during training.

Persistence is facilitated if fairly fresh cross-tracks are left out and only those older than the initial one are used. On the dog's arrival at a cross-track, he must be given a chance to learn how to distinguish its smell from that of the initial track. For this purpose he must smell the cross-tracks, for otherwise he cannot register the differences of scent. The smelling of human cross-tracks—not of course of those of animals—is, therefore, necessary. But on each occasion the dog's behaviour, as it smells and compares scents, must be closely watched.

Such reaction to scent difference as we can see does not begin, in the case of a fully trained dog, until the animal has followed the scent of the cross-track for a short distance. His initial behaviour does not therefore indicate whether the dog has made an erroneous change-over to the cross-track and is following its scent, or whether he may yet reject the false track. The dog may be merely testing the quality of the scent of the cross-track. The answer will depend on whether after this test he turns of his own accord, thus abandoning the cross-track, and spontaneously takes up the initial track again, or whether he continues to follow the cross-track, not declining its scent but pursuing it exactly as he would that of the initial track.

A dog that has still to learn that it should decline strange tracks will at first, especially when differences in age are slight, change over to them and follow them up methodically. The main object of training is to break him of this habit.

Here the question arises to what distance the dog should be allowed to test the strange track, to give him time to register the difference of scent, while preventing him from taking up and working out the cross-track. It may be observed that the shorter the time difference between initial and cross-track, the more intensive will be the smelling of the cross-tracks, thus the longer the delay and the greater the distance covered during testing. It follows that the trainer must freely permit the smelling and testing of cross-tracks. He should only interfere when it is evident that the dog has taken up the cross-track and is working it out. If age difference is slight, a novice dog should be allowed at most ten paces to test a strange cross-track.

The choice of ground in practising with cross-tracks is of great importance. A ground on which the dog is given the chance to use his memory in addition to his nose for finding is unsuitable. The course and its conclusion must always be so arranged that recollection of events during previous exercises cannot be turned to advantage. This can be done by working in territory where a very large number of cross-tracks run together in disorderly fashion within the scenting area of the course (though not at the start of the initial track) while the latter is always so arranged as to differ as regards length, direction, corners, curves and conclusion from that of its predecessor.

We have still to consider how persistence on the initial track can be facilitated for the dog at an early stage. An individual scent laid by a series of footprints can only be held by a track-

sure dog if the track runs for some distance and in isolated
fashion into the surrounding territory, so that the scent in
question remains for a certain length of time free from other
human track-scents. A strong scent for the initial track is, therefore, established at the starting-point. The track-layer walks

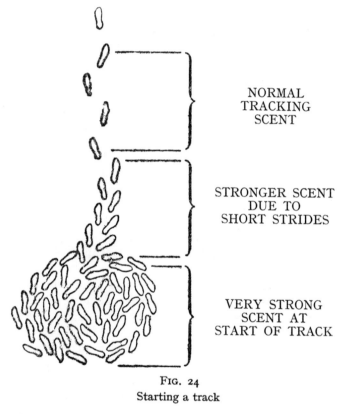

NORMAL
TRACKING
SCENT

STRONGER SCENT
DUE TO
SHORT STRIDES

VERY STRONG
SCENT AT
START OF TRACK

Fig. 24
Starting a track

to and fro for one or two minutes, without scraping up the
ground, in an area of about half a square yard. Then he paces
the first ten steps of the track in very short strides, thereafter resuming his normal stride (*see* Fig. 24). This method of
starting the track begins from the very first day and from this
the dog will proceed by stages from a powerfully scented area
to the degree of strength provided by the normal track. A
thorough scenting of the olfactory field at the start of the track

is important. It is effected firstly by the strength of the initial scent and secondly by the fact that the continuation of the track is not laid in the direction in which the trainer sets the animal. The dog is therefore obliged to search the scent-area for an outlet and consequently has to work it thoroughly.

These formal arrangements should make it clear to the trainer how important it is to teach the dog to make a thorough exploration of the track-scent right at the start of the track. An essential condition for success in practical tracking work is the presence of enough olfactory stimuli at the start of the track to enable the dog to become familiar, at this early stage, with the specific track-scent left behind by the maker of the track. It will then be possible for the dog, from the start of the track, to follow this specific track-scent across other human tracks, even those of the same age or fresher. If the trainer is obliged to set his dog at only one footprint, the animal will then need a fairly long stretch, which may be from thirty to sixty yards, depending on the nature of the ground, before it can pick up the quantity of olfactory stimuli required to render it familiar with the track-scent. If this section of the track should be cut by fairly recent cross-tracks, especially at acute angles, or blocked to any extent in its course, the success of tracking is likely to be imperilled.

The trainer must also teach his dog to track when only a small quantity of olfactory stimuli are available at the start of the track. This, for example, would be the case if there were only a single footprint at the starting-point. As has already been stressed, it is most essential in laying tracks to make sure at the first lesson that both the start of the track and all the details of its course are precisely known to the trainer. As soon as tracks exceed fifty paces a number of objects are set down, always at irregular intervals and never less than fifty paces apart.

Not until the track has been laid does the trainer fetch the dog from its position at a distance and lead it close up to the start of the track. The tracking-harness is now adjusted and the line fitted. These manipulations, always carried out in the same way, come in time to form, with the word 'Seek', a secondary inducement or commencement signal, and consequently an incentive to the picking up and following of the track. This procedure is of special value in cases when, as on active service, the starting-point of the track is unknown to the trainer or handler.

Training begins with the dog, as mentioned in Section (c), being held on a short lead, lengthened as soon as the animal begins to smell over the start of the track, to the sound of 'There's a good boy' and 'Seek', accompanied by the gestures appropriate to tracking. A dog which may at once dash forward is followed at a normal pace. The remaining inducements are noted in Section (c). Any erroneous attitude of the dog to the track-scent, whether by using sight, keeping the nose high, listening, picking up animal or other scents which may attract it in any way and so on, must be repressed. The severity of the correction may be increased proportionately as the dog's ability to track improves. The encouragements given when an object is found must, however, be all the stronger, so that the animal's pleasure in the work may be constantly renewed and intensified.

If the dog works out training tracks with two corners about 100 yards in length satisfactorily, the number of corners is increased—their direction being constantly changed—and the tracks are gradually brought up to 400 yards in length (see Figs. 25 and 26). The inclusion of several angles encourages the incessant use of the nose, for the many abrupt changes of direction enforce a lasting tension and impose greater strain on the power of scent. If the dog over-runs a corner, the trainer at once stands still and watches the animal. If the dog starts hunting instead of searching for the lost track-scent, the trainer applies inducement by means of the lead and the word 'Seek'. The main point is that the dog should learn to decline strange track-scents. With a track-length of about 400 yards the age of the track may be about an hour.

When the dogs have reached the track-sure stage, when they can be relied on to follow the initial track without switching to fresher or older cross-tracks, initial tracks are gradually increased to about a mile and a quarter. Work is then taken to a different territory.

This transfer is first arranged by starting the tracks on the ground hitherto used for training and continuing them on territory unfamiliar to the dog, where they are laid over paths and roads, including built-up areas and those used by pedestrians and vehicles. In this way the animals are not only kept

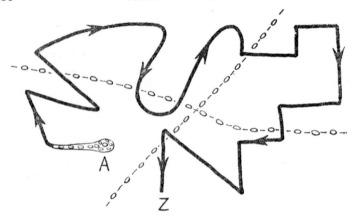

A   BEGINNING OF TRACK
Z   END OF TRACK
o—o—o   CROSS TRACKS

Fig. 25
Example of track

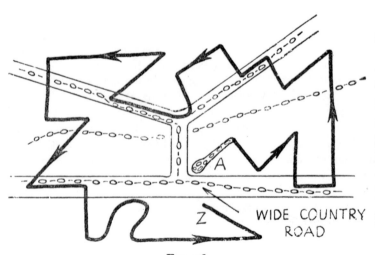

Fig. 26
Example of track

concentrated on their task of declining cross-tracks but are also familiarized with other distractions of an olfactory, auditory and visual character, due to pedestrian and vehicular traffic.

When an advanced stage of tracking is reached, tracks may be gradually extended up to two and a half miles, and their age increased to about three hours. Trainers have eventually to become accustomed to tracking work in which they are entirely ignorant of the courses laid and are obliged themselves to provide the starting-point. An accurately drawn plan showing the course of the track must be available to enable inducements to be applied to the dog and, in this case, to the trainer as well. The trainer being entirely ignorant of the course, now learns for the first time to make certain observations regarding his dog's behaviour which formerly often escaped his notice. He learns, for example, to judge much more accurately whether the dog is following the initial track or not. Since, however, the dog is still at the novice stage, he must only be allowed freedom while he sticks to the initial track and declines strange ones. If the dog slackens in making this effort, the instructor must immediately notify the trainer to that effect and the latter must at once intervene. At this point, if the dog again assumes the undesirable attitude, work will continue with the instructor keeping the trainer acquainted with the course of the track. For the main point is now the prompt application of inducements to the dog under instruction. Work on the usual training ground must also be continually repeated and tracks of a thoroughly complex character be laid there and worked out by the dog, if necessary, under compulsion. At a certain stage of learning many dogs work extremely well under compulsion. But they cease to do so when given a considerable degree of freedom in tracking, for example if the trainer does not know the course of the track they are on. In the case of these dogs compulsion has not yet had its full effect and for the time being further compulsive inducements must be applied while working on tracks the course of which is known to the trainer.

On active service consistently reliable performance can only be achieved by a trainer whose dog has learnt to work out a track, even in the absence of compulsion, by a most painstaking use of the nose. Such is the object of training, and in order to achieve it compulsion must have been previously employed for

N

an adequate time. The excuse that 'my dog is not in the mood for tracking today' will not do and would not be necessary had training been properly carried out. There must, of course, be a frequent return to compulsive inducement on the training ground. It is quite a different matter if the dog is unable to pick up the track of a malefactor at the scene of the crime owing to the place having been visited by other people, or to the track being so old that it can no longer afford sufficient traces of scent for the dog's nose to work on. In such a case, of course, the failure to pick up a track cannot be held to discredit either the dog or his trainer.

Training at this stage is more and more assimilated to the conditions of active service. Tracks are no longer started on the training ground but beyond it. Wooded country and isolated houses give both trainer and dog good opportunities for following tracks. 'Burglaries', for example, may be staged in isolated houses, outbuildings, etc. Tracks are laid from such points, the dog and its handler arriving there hours afterwards. In this connection it may be added that in practice success has never yet been achieved in the detection of robberies which have taken place on other than ground floors. Apparently, so little scent is left on wood that the trail cannot be picked up. Tracks also have to be worked out in the dark. It is important in such cases to keep the dog under observation to take note of any significant movements he may make. A pocket torch carried by the trainer is not much use, for the beam must be at least ten yards long to illuminate the ground in front of the dog, since the dog's handler must be able to observe the territory ahead as well as the animal's own pursuit action. It would also be impossible in such instances to follow every movement by the dog, as one would have to be constantly directing the torch upon the animal. An illuminated harness, which can be used when dogs are put on the track, has been found effective. This harness is fitted with a lamp that throws a diagonal beam forwards and downwards. It illuminates about four square yards of ground in such a way that the handler can not only see his dog but also discern all the necessary ground indications. Whichever way the dog turns the beam always points forward and adequately illuminates the ground immediately in front of the animal. The handler himself remains in the dark but is enabled to follow the dog with certainty and without dashing about. Moreover, he has his hands free to deal with any possible eventualities.

Some hints may be added for the handler of track-sure dogs. It may happen on very long tracks that dogs become reluctant, owing to overstrain, to go on working. If the signs of such overstrain are noticed a note should be taken of the place at which the dog was still hot on the track, and the animal allowed to rest for about a quarter of an hour. When a fresh start is made a well-trained animal will immediately pick up the track again and resume work. If the track being followed by the dog is interrupted at a certain point, where the ground might be paved or much frequented, an attempt must either be made to get the dog itself to resume the track, or, if this expedient is impracticable, the handler himself must undertake the task.

Finally, it should again be emphasized that the track-sure dog neither follows the individual human scent on a track nor gives notice of conformities in scent between track and object or track and man. He follows the specific scent given off by a track of a certain age and takes note of all objects contained within the scent-range of the track if they bear scent of human type. The individual human scent, therefore, plays no part in this process.

CHAPTER X

FAMILIARIZATION WITH DISTURBANCES— WORK IN WATER—"SPEAKING"

1. FAMILIARIZATION WITH DISTURBANCES

THE decisive method for securing reliability on active service is to familiarize the dog with all the experiences that may occur on such service and, if possible, to include in the programme all the disturbances which might conceivably arise. The purpose for which the animal will be used must, therefore, be our guide in considering with what kind of disturbances he should be made familiar. Here noises, particularly those made by firearms, are of special importance.

Dogs cannot, of course, be trained to show courage and contempt of death. We are, on the contrary, obliged to represent the noises they hear as harmless, so that we may achieve our object of making them perform their work without suspecting any danger. Training, therefore, should not resemble active service in exposing the dog to drastic unpleasantness in the shape of pain or alarm. Otherwise undesirable associations will be initiated between the noises heard and the reactions of pain or alarm, with the consequence that when such noises are repeated the dog will experience extreme fright and be prejudiced in its work or even rendered useless.

This view may appear to be contradicted by the fact that dogs are not necessarily frightened by a noise even after they have received some hurt at the same time. But what happens, in such cases, is simply that no association between the two has been formed. This may occur when the wound does not instantly give rise to pain, or when no loud noise coincides with the pain.

We cannot achieve our object by compulsion, for that would merely establish undesirable associations—such as that a noise is connected with something unpleasant.

The behaviour of untrained dogs when shots are fired varies. To ascertain what it may be, an assistant should fire a single pistol or revolver shot several dozen paces away from the trainer while the dog is held by the trainer on the lead. If the animal shows fear, it should be stroked, while repeated sounds of encouragement are uttered, and played with. If it tries to get away from the explosion, it should be allowed, with the same encouraging inducements, to retreat to a distance at which it no longer shows any fear. The animal should never be dragged towards the location of the report. The object of training can only be attained by encouragement leading to the realization that the report does not do any harm. When the dog ceases to show fear, the distance from the source of the noise is steadily reduced. In this way police dogs are familiarized with the sounds of various types of firearm.

Barking must be repressed right from the start and exciting accompanying circumstances avoided. The best plan is to ensure that the dog has only agreeable experiences while the noises are proceeding. If when single shots are fired close to it the animal remains quiet and unconcerned, the sounds are made louder, for instance by the simultaneous firing of a number of shots. The following disturbances, with which the service dog should be made familiar, may be listed: noises by single individuals, groups, columns on the march, heavy lorries, buses, trains, horsemen, cyclists, places of amusement, strange dogs and other animals. To these we may add fog, bad weather (snow, rain and wind), difficulties of terrain (mountains, forests with undergrowth, marshes), obstacles (trenches, hedges, fences, walls of stone or wood, barbed wire, watercourses, lakes, shelters, etc.) The next step will be training in darkness. So far as possible disturbances of the same character as those used by day will be included. Any lights visible should be taken into consideration.

Always remember that fear is invariably increased by compulsion. Fear can only be eliminated by fondling and encouragement as well as by showing the animals that the disturbances do not cause them pain.

2. WORK IN WATER

A dog usually only becomes shy of water owing to erroneous handling. The first rule is never to employ any strict compulsion. A dog will get into a pitiable state of terror of water if he is pushed or thrown into it. A warm summer day affords the best opportunity for familiarizing the dog with water. It is then impelled by the heat to seek coolness and moisture. At first, smooth, still water only should be used. It should be of such depth that the dog can touch the bottom with its feet. A pool with gently sloping banks is particularly suitable. Matters are facilitated if the trainer himself goes in the water. Another dog, laready used to the water, is also helpful, provided he gets on well with the dog under instruction.

At first 'paddling' in smooth water is practised. The trainer is not present in the character of an overseer but in that of an animal-loving spectator. It is important that at the start of the exercise the period spent in the water should be brief. It is also important to allow the animal plenty of free movement after each lesson so that he should never be put on the lead immediately afterwards. On the dog's return home, still rather wet, he must be rubbed thoroughly dry and given a resting-place free from draughts; otherwise he may easily catch cold.

After a few repetitions of the training, most dogs will enter the water of their own accord in hot weather. A number of methods are used to accustom the animals to deeper water and to induce them to swim. There is no point in making up one's mind that the dog has got to learn to swim on any particular day. One should be quite satisfied if he only goes a little deeper into the water than he did in the previous exercise. Use can be made of the pleasure the dog takes in retrieving. Another inducement may take the form of the trainer leaving the bank by boat, the dog remaining ashore, preferably in company with another dog that can already swim, and then encouraging the pupil to come to him. Again, one may go to the other side of a wide ditch, which the dog cannot jump, and leave him to be held by an assistant till called.

Dogs do not at first swim properly, but 'paddle'. The fore-paws generally strike the water instead of pulling through it. This kind of swimming, in which the dog still feels fear, requires a great deal of effort. The dog, in his clumsiness as a novice, uses a number of muscles which would not be called into play by an experienced swimmer, just as a human beginner does. Consequently, work in water is at first very fatiguing for the animal. The preliminary swimming lessons should, therefore, last only a short time and should only take place in still water.

Not until the dog is swimming quite confidently and quietly, with its forepaws no longer out of the water, should training be undertaken in running water.

3. "Speaking"

Auditory signal: 'Bark'.

To train a dog to speak at a certain signal, every opportunity should be taken of observing when the dog, of its own accord, in response to some primary inducement, barks, yelps, whines, howls, whimpers, growls or snarls. The sound 'Bark' should then be uttered, while the right arm is bent and raised and lowered as far as chest level. If the dog is close to one's side, the upper part of the body should simultaneously be inclined forwards. As these signals should not provoke any kind of hostility, the primary inducements which cause that behaviour by the dog should not be applied in conjunction with the auditory signal 'Bark' and the visual signals that accompany it.

The following are some examples of primary inducements which do not result in the adoption of a hostile attitude.

If one holds out the dish containing the animal's meal or some particularly tasty morsel, he will often begin to whine. If he is left alone in the kennel or elsewhere for some considerable time, he will, when the trainer approaches, greet him with loud expressions of joy, and whine in depressed fashion when the trainer again goes away. The dog will also whine if he is tied up in a lonely place and his handler then runs away, calling him, and after reaching a certain distance begins running to and fro. Active movements by the trainer are especially calculated in such circumstances to increase considerably the dog's impulse to start whining.

On all occasions when he succeeds in provoking the animal to utter even a few sounds, the trainer should give the call 'Bark', accompanying it from time to time with the sound of encouragement, and simultaneously raise and lower to chest level the crooked right arm while bending the upper part of the body forward. In this way the ground will be prepared for the formation, by memory, of an association betwen the reaction of barking and the secondary inducements applied. If the dog is immediately released from isolation or immediately given the food held out, the moment he utters even a few sounds, the ground is prepared for the further association that barking is followed by release from isolation or by eating. This experience will also serve to increase the excitement that heightens the dog's inclination to begin giving tongue.

Many dogs need a long period of training before they will speak on secondary inducements alone.

We must remember that neither the call 'Bark' nor the physical gestures of the trainer in any sense imply a command. The dog does not understand the reason for the exercise and merely reacts to certain sense-stimuli. We must, therefore, repeatedly return to primary inducements and their associated signals.

The inexperienced trainer should never use compulsion in the early stages. On the contrary, during the first weeks of training he should only practise giving tongue if the dog is in the mood to co-operate. Inducements to bark should cease directly they are found to be unsuccessful.

Not until the dog has started to respond satisfactorily to the secondary inducement 'Bark' and the visual signals should compulsion begin and then it should only take a mild form. The sound 'Bark' when of an admonitory character, should be followed by 'There's a good boy' the moment the dog gives any signs of beginning to speak.

It will be useful for the understanding of the true nature of training to call attention to an undesirable association which, though not inevitable, may easily arise during training in giving tongue.

When the dog for purposes of isolation is tied to a tree, it will soon be perceived that at first it is necessary for the trainer to be a certain distance away before the sounds required are elicited. A nearer approach will cause the animal's feeling of isolation to weaken or disappear, so that he will not bark. The experience of being released immediately after giving tongue will, by degrees, cause response at a reduced distance and finally even when the trainer comes close to the dog or merely calls 'Bark' directly after tying him up.

All these intermediate steps should be regarded as advances. The trainer's eventual aim is to make the animal speak without being tied up. It may refuse for the reason that isolation must at first depend upon the sense-stimulus of the call 'Bark' being uttered while a tree is in view; both these stimuli being required together in order to produce the desired attitude. Without the visual stimulus 'tree' what we desire will not happen. The behaviour required may be proved by taking the dog close up to a tree. He will then bark. Intensification of the exercise will, therefore, consist in gradually increasing the distance between the dog and trees. In this way the stimulus 'Bark' will be detached from the tree association until it is effective when used alone.

This procedure is also applicable to training in giving tongue carried out at the kennel.

CHAPTER XI

TRAINING AND MANAGEMENT OF SERVICE DOGS

IT NEVER occurs to anyone merely to study a manual on riding and then mount an unbroken horse in order to break it in. The animal's powerful physique prevents such action. Horses are broken in by specialists in riding technique. Not until they have been thoroughly broken are they mounted by those who are learning to ride and the lessons proceed under the direction of a riding-master. As a rule matters are arranged differently with dogs. They are not so strong, unfortunately, as horses. Accordingly, a dog is put on the lead straight away and marched off, while his human companion behaves from the start like an omniscient master, though he may, in fact, know little or nothing of the subject of training. The physical superiority of a man to a dog makes it easy to forget that the man is also a pupil and to fail to realize that the relationship of man to dog is a more difficult one than that of man to horse. The dog is the only domestic animal in the employment of man in which psychological, in addition to physical, attributes are turned to account. For this reason the necessity for expert knowledge in the training and management of dogs is even more essential than in the breaking of horses. An animal like a horse, which is used almost exclusively as a mechanical instrument, is far easier to control than one in which psychological as well as physical factors have to be taken into account and applied to practical purposes.

Reliable canine services are secured with the greatest certainty and speed by putting a dog into the hands of human pupils and then instructing and guiding them together in the necessary technique. A complete misconception of the technical position is revealed by the disdainful description given of the courses organized for the training of dog-handlers in various service establishments in Germany, when they are referred to as pressure courses which spoil far more dogs than they teach.

These courses are concerned primarily with education in the management of dogs and it can be affirmed without exaggeration that their organization implies so decisive an advance in this field that the methodical employment of service dogs would be unthinkable without it. Reliable canine services had, it is true, been secured at an earlier date by individual trainers who had spent years in painfully acquiring the necessary knowledge and experience. Participants in the present-day courses can attain this technical standard in a few weeks under expert tuition. A second important advantage is that the apprentice trainer is taught to apply the right inducements to the dog from the very start of the course. Consequently, and as a result of the lessons in training being based upon the proper technical foundations, the dog learns far more quickly and accurately than would be the case if it were individually instructed by an inexperienced trainer. In a single course of eight weeks so much progress can be made in the education of handlers and the training of dogs that the animals can be taken straight into service. The achievement of this result does, of course, involve a very thorough exploitation of time and space. Each handler and his dog are permanently under supervision and training proceeds, so to speak, on the conveyor belt system. Not a moment is allowed to pass unused. Training lasts for four hours every day. At the warm season of the year it takes place in early morning or in late afternoon. An area of some sixty acres is required and divided into five training grounds: fifty pupils with fifty dogs are taught by five training-masters and five assistants in plain clothes. The assistants are chosen from among the pupils, changed daily and not accompanied by their dogs.

Ground 1 is the place of assembly for teachers, pupils and dogs, where they collect for the start and where they assemble again at the conclusion of the day's work.

Four teachers with one assistant each occupy Grounds 2 to 5, one teacher with one assistant remaining on Ground 1. The assistants act partly as observers and partly as auxiliary trainers, at first under the teacher's direction and later independently, e.g. in man-work, in self-defence by the dog, in track-laying. They thus receive first-rate instruction, many dogs passing through their hands every day. Moreover, the dogs themselves have the obvious advantage, as they learn, of the daily change of assistants.

At the same time as the teachers and assistants go to the various Grounds, two pupils with their dogs leave Ground 1 for each of the Grounds 2 to 5, thus leaving on Ground 1, in addition to one teacher and his assistant, thirty-seven pupils and their dogs. One pupil with his dog trains on each of Grounds 2 to 5, while the second pupil stands ready to begin in his turn. On Ground 3, until the fourteenth day of training, five or six pupils can be working at the same time. At this Ground the teacher and his assistant go from one training pitch to another. Self-defence is only taught at pitches where the teacher and his assistant are present. At the other pitches the dogs are simply familiarized with isolation. Arrival at and departure from Ground 3 are regulated by summonses from the teacher at 1 to the teacher at 3.

Each pupil, on concluding his exercise, leaves Ground 2 for Ground 3 and for the first fourteen days leaves Ground 3 for either 4 or 5, man-work only being undertaken once a day. Pupils leaving the Grounds where this work proceeds go back direct to Ground 1.

Each pupil, on returning to Ground 1, reports to the teacher there, who at once despatches replacements to the other Grounds. On the fifteenth day a change in the programme is instituted. Training on Grounds 3 to 5 then consists of man-work, together with subordination training or reconnaissance. Consequently the teacher at Ground 1 can send pupils direct to any Ground from which men are reporting back to him.

As to individual Grounds we may observe that the properties required to break dogs of the habits of picking up food, eating refuse and rolling in it are scattered over all Grounds. It is desirable that Ground 1 should include, in addition to the distractions provided by the large number of dogs at exercise, other types of distractions such as pedestrians, vehicles, tracks and droppings of game, etc.

Ground 1 should be as easy to survey as possible. It needs a scale jump with a number of boards, adjustable to heights between one and a half feet and six feet, and at least one six foot wall as well as growing hedges for the clear jump and, if possible, several different types of obstacle, such as meshed wire fencing about four feet high, various sloping-sided trenches of about three feet in depth and five to nine feet wide, and water suitable for swimming.

Ground 2 is primarily used for compulsive retrieving by dogs found by the teacher to be lacking in aptitude for retrieving in play. Eight days will be enough to make all dogs reliable in compulsive retrieving and the Ground can then be used for tracking by dogs which, by special request, are being given tracking instruction despite the fact that they are actually guard dogs.

At Ground 3 five or six posts are driven into the earth, each having a six foot long chain attached, fitted with a spring and a wide, specially strong leather collar. No post is visible from the position of any other and they are widely enough separated to preclude exercises from interfering with one another. After fourteen days self-defence training will be brought to the desired level of efficiency and Ground 3, like Grounds 4 and 5, will then be used for man-work.

When thirty-four working days have passed both handlers and dogs are far enough advanced for the last fourteen days to be devoted to preparing both for entry into service.

Exercises then include prolonged reconnaissance of human beings and objects over large areas, five minutes' uninterrupted baying and the retrieving of lost and hidden objects, bearing human scent, of weights up to ten pounds. The taking into custody of single individuals and of groups, prevention of the flight of groups or individuals and the release of groups or individuals cornered by the dog, are also practised, together with the searching of empty and full barns, lofts, cellars, depositories, dwelling-houses and other likely hiding-places of the kind.

There are also at least four exercises in darkness, during which the dogs are provided with illuminated harness. In these exercises the same services, such as are required on active duty, are expected as by daylight.

All training is carried out under conditions involving continuous change of location beyond the training grounds with which the dog is already familiar.

INDEX

ABSTENTION training, 28 *et seq.*, 47 *et seq.*

Action training, 31 *et seq.*, 47 *et seq.*

Air and scent, 162

Alarm, exercises involving, 92 (*see also* Fear)

Anthropomorphism, 20

Appetite, 102

Arrest procedure, 143 *et seq.*

Association, 41, 42

——, undesirable, 21, 23, 24, 55, 66

Attacks by dogs, 35, 36

—— by captives, 144, 145

Auditory stimulus, 19, 47

BACKWARD run, 83 *et seq.*, 87, 88, 92

Bark as quarry, 182

Barking, baying, 128, 135, 136, 142, 143, 147, 156, 193, 195 *et seq.*

Body-scent, track-scent, 160, 164, 167, 168, 170 (*see also* Scent)

Böttger, 163, 172, 180

Bounding, 53

Burglary, upper floors, 190

Busch, W., 73

Buttons as objects, 182

CANINE Research Society, 7

Capture of criminals, 123 *et seq.*, 141 *et seq.*

Chain, the casting, 91, 92, 103

Character, 37, 38

"Cleverness", 38

Clothing, protective, 127, 131, 139 *et seq.*

Collars, 26, 50, 56, 118 *et seq.*, 129, 173

Colour and tracking objects, 178

Compulsion principles, 24, 25, 26 *et seq.*, 35 *et seq.*, 82, 117 *et seq.*, 189, 190 (*see also* Discipline)

"Cornering", 146 *et seq.*, 151

Courses for handlers, 198, 199

Cross-tracks, 183 *et seq.*

DARKNESS, training in, 190, 193, 201

Deerskins, 128

Depression, 78, 79, 87, 127, 128, 129

Discipline, 50 *et seq.* (*see also* Compulsion)

"Disciplinary shot", 90, 91

Distractions, disturbances, 24, 39, 171, 192, 193

"Down" training, 34, 48, 55, 62 *et seq.*, 86

Dropping, 68 *et seq.*

Dumb-bells, 101, 109 *et seq.*

EXCREMENT, rolling in, 102

FALLS, by captives, 145

Fear, 39, 52, 73 *et seq.*, 92, 193 (*see also* Timidity)

Feeding rules, 104 *et seq.*

Fighting, in packs, 35

Food, refusal of, 102 *et seq.*

Footprints, 158, 184, 185, 186

Footwear scents, 158

Forepaw injury, 100

Freedom, harmful effects of, 106

Frost and scent, 162

GERMAN Society for Animal Psychology, 7

Gestures as commands, 21 *et seq.*

Grass, scent on, 162
Ground, for training, 39, 155, 170, 171, 181, 184, 187, 188, 190
Guard duties, 123 et seq.
Guarding of objects, 130
Gunfire, 192, 193

HAND-SHYNESS, 35, 71
Harness, 180, 190
Heel on lead, 34, 50, 57
Height of jumps, 100
Heredity, 37
Hunting, 28, 29, 73, 157, 187

ILLUMINATION, night training, 190, 201
Indoor training, 39, 87, 108, 109
Inducements, 19 et seq., 26 et seq., 84
Instincts, 37, 38, 72, 84
Intelligence, 21, 22, 94
Intimidation, 39, 40, 48, 52
Introduction to Dog Training, quoted, 162, 163

JUMPING, 98 et seq., 200
—— scale, 99, 100, 200
Justus-Liebig Technical College, 8

KINDNESS, compulsion, in training, 24, 25, 93 (see also Compulsion)

LEAD training, 50 et seq., 82, 89, 90, 149, 178 et seq.
Leather, 158, 174, 178
Length of tracks, 187 et seq.
Licking, 93

Max and Moritz, 73
Meetings between dogs, 96
Memory, 22, 40, 41, 94

Moving ahead, 53, 58, 59
Muzzle angle in tracking, 157, 164, 167, 168, 170, 172

NIGHT work, 190, 193, 201
Noise, reaction to, 192, 193
North German Dog Farm, 7, 8
Nose positions in tracking (see under Muzzle)

OBJECTS, tracking of, 157, 161, 163, 171, 172 (see also Retrieving)
Outdoor training, 39
Overnight tracks, 162
Over-shooting, over-running, 168 et seq., 172, 176, 177, 179, 187

PACE acceleration, 49
Pack instinct, 72, 84
Pavements and scent, 182
"Perversity", 85
Police work, 123 et seq.
Pressure courses, 198, 199
Psychology, animal, 7, 17 et seq., 198
Punishment, 25, 26 et seq., 36, 68, 69, 93
Pursuit training, 137, 140 et seq.

QUARTERING, 156

RAIN and scent, 162
Rank in packs, 72
Recall training, 50, 62 et seq., 71 et seq., 96
Reconnaissance, 154 et seq.
Refuse, 102, 103
Resistance, 35, 36, 87
Retrieving:
    associations, undesirable, 116, 117
    compulsion, 117 et seq.

Retrieving (*cont.*):
drill, 110
dropping, premature, 115, 116
environmental stimuli, 108
general considerations, 106 *et seq.*
objects, 109, 112, 122, 175, 176
(*see also* Objects)
over jumps, 101
picking up, 113, 114
recall, 113
sitting, 112, 113
snatching, 111
Rewards, 27, 40, 52
Run, the backward, 83 *et seq.*, 87, 88, 92
Running ahead, 49

SANDY ground, scent on, 161
Scent, 35, 154, 155, 157 *et seq.*, 161 *et seq.*, 164 *et seq.*, 190, 191
Self-control, 84
Self-defence (dogs), 129 *et seq.*
Sense stimulus, 18 *et seq.*
Signals, 21 *et seq.*, 47 *et seq.*, 93
Sitting, 59, 60
Snow; effect on scent, 162
"Speaking", 195
Standing, 55, 65, 66, 67, 97, 98
Stick, attack by, 152
Sticks, training, 133 *et seq.*, 152, 153
"Stupidity", 38
Sunset and tracks, 162
Sunshine and scent, 162
Surfaces, tracking, 161, 162
Swimming, 194, 195
Switches, 26, 36, 68, 69

TIME interval, track selection, 161, 162, 178, 187, 189
Timidity, 123, 124 (*see also* Fear)
Toe injuries, 101
Traces, 181

Tracks, tracking:
cross, 183 *et seq.*
design, 179, 187 *et seq.*
fidelity, 159, 160, 161, 173
general considerations, 157 *et seq.*
human, 158 *et seq.*
lengths, 187 *et seq.*
muzzle angle, 157, 164, 167, 168, 170, 172
off lead, 175 *et seq.*
sureness, 161, 173, 180 *et seq.*, 187, 191
track-scents, 157, 158, 160, 164
track-happy dogs, 160, 171, 172 *et seq.*, 178 *et seq.*
Training, aims of, 23, 42, 43, 95
—— sites, 39, 155, 170, 171 181, 184, 187, 188, 190
Tutorial and Experimental Inst. for Armed Forces Dogs, 7
Twigs, for training, 182

VEGETATION, scent on, 162
Visual stimulus, 41, 47

WAR training, 7
Water, work in, 193 *et seq.*
Welcome, importance of, 93 (*see also* Kindness)
Wet surfaces and scent, 161
Whips, whipping, 25, 26 *et seq.*, 36, 68, 69, 93
Whistling, 95
Wind, 135, 162, 164 *et seq.*, 174, 176, 177
Wood and scent, 190
Wooded country as training area, 190

ZIG-ZAG tracks, 171